WOMEN IN BLUE

Other Books in the Women of Action Series

WOMEN IN BLUE

···

16 Brave Officers, Forensics Experts, Police Chiefs, and More

CHERYL MULLENBACH

CHICAGO
REVIEW
PRESS

Copyright © 2016 by Cheryl Mullenbach
All rights reserved
First hardcover edition published in 2016
First paperback edition published in 2024
Published by Chicago Review Press Incorporated
814 North Franklin Street
Chicago, Illinois 60610
ISBN 978-0-89733-306-1

The Library of Congress has cataloged the hardcover edition
as follows:
Mullenbach, Cheryl, author.
Women in blue : 16 Brave Officers, Forensics Experts, Police
Chiefs, and More / Cheryl Mullenbach.
pages cm
Includes bibliographical references and index.
ISBN 978-1-61373-422-3 (cloth : alk. paper) 1. Policewomen—
United States—Case studies. 2. Law enforcement—United
States I. Title.

HV8023.M856 2016
363.2092'520973—dc23

2015032406

Cover and interior design: Sarah Olson
Cover photos: (top) torbakhopper/scott richard; (bottom,
    left to right) Sadie Likens, courtesy Sam Howe Collection,
    Mss. 00199 (Scan #10027002), History Colorado, Denver,
    Colorado; Julia Grimes, courtesy Julia Grimes; Cristina Pino,
    courtesy Christina Pino; Frances Glessner Lee, courtesy
    Glessner House Museum, Chicago, IL

Printed in the United States of America

Always for Richard L. Wohlgamuth

CONTENTS

....

AUTHOR'S NOTE

....

THE WOMEN PROFILED in this book are brave law enforcement personnel and deal with difficult, dangerous, and at times violent situations. Some of these experiences are recounted in the text. Although I have attempted to include age-appropriate content and resources, I recommend adult guidance for younger readers.

INTRODUCTION

· · · · · · · · · · · · · ·

THE MAYOR OF LORAIN, Ohio, made his opinion of police-women perfectly clear in the *Rock Island Argus* newspaper in 1907: "Huh! A good joke . . . dressed in picture hats and peeka-boo waists patrolling the streets in search of criminals!"

Faced with such attitudes, women who wanted to work in law enforcement broke through numerous barriers. Some male chiefs refused to hire them; some male coworkers snubbed them. The public didn't always take them seriously. There seemed to be more interest in their clothing styles than any merit they offered in curbing crime.

They were called guardettes, copettes, and police in petti-coats in the early 1900s. It would be a long time before women in law enforcement were known simply as law enforcement officials.

The evolution of titles and attitudes spans over 150 years. The first women involved in official police work were prison and jail matrons. New York's Auburn prison hired a matron in

Male and female officers demonstrating handcuff techniques.
Library of Congress, LC-USZ62-116714

1832, but it was slow going for the next century as police departments were reluctant to employ females in any capacity other than cleaners, laundresses, and cooks.

It took pressure from women's organizations—most notably the Woman's Christian Temperance Union (WCTU)—to force police departments to employ women as protectors of women and children and as law enforcers. In the mid- to late 1800s cities across the country, including Chicago, Detroit, and Philadelphia, hired matrons.

By the early 1900s those matrons (and again women's organizations) began to pressure city leaders to be more equitable to women in law enforcement. They demanded better pay and expanded job duties. As they began to acquire those, their titles changed to *policewoman* and their roles revolved around being social workers and protectors of women and children. They were the city's mothers and guardians.

It wasn't until the early 1970s, when the women's movement impacted the workplace—including police work—that the title of *police officer* applied to all officers regardless of gender. The law guaranteed equality for women in law enforcement. Women should have been treated with equality—patrolling the streets in a squad car, wearing sensible uniforms, carrying and using weapons, competing for advancement, heading departments. But equality was not automatic merely because of the law. In many cases, women had to sue to realize those rights.

In 1913 a newspaper reporter asked, "If the hand of the law were to descend heavily on your shoulder, would it make any difference to you whether the hand was attached to a round, feminine arm or to an angular, hairy masculine limb?"

If the question were posed today, would the answer be different than in 1913?

PART I

BREAKING INTO JAIL

═══════════════════════

The Early Matrons

IN 1826 RACHEL WELCH was being held in solitary confinement in Auburn Prison in New York when she became pregnant. She died after a flogging by a prison official.

Anna was a teenager locked in a Chicago jail in 1915. The only toilet available for female prisoners was located in a hall where male jailers made lewd comments as they watched the female prisoners use the facilities.

Over the years female prisoners experienced these and countless other atrocities in the nation's police stations, jails, and prisons. In the early and mid-1800s very few women worked in these penal institutions. Women prisoners were housed in close proximity to men in institutions where male officials searched them and jailers and other prisoners often subjected them to sexual abuse.

Hidden behind the walls of jails and prisons and out of sight of the average citizen, these women had no voice. However, many of them were in jail for drunkenness, and they drew the attention of the Woman's Christian Temperance Union (WCTU), a group that worked for the elimination of the consumption of alcohol. When the WCTU women visited the jails and saw conditions, they were shocked. While alcohol was their original concern, prison reform soon became a focus.

The WCTU was formed in 1874, and when Frances Willard became president in 1879 the organization's work expanded beyond the realm of temperance. Her motto was "Do everything." They advocated for suffrage, on behalf of child workers, and for labor's right to organize. It was through the pressure of the WCTU that many cities hired their first jail matrons. Finally incarcerated women had a voice outside the walls.

Along the path toward introducing matrons into the penal system, there was resistance from municipal leaders and police department heads—most of whom were men. These officials claimed that female matrons would not be able to handle unruly female prisoners. But the most common excuse was that the city budget couldn't accommodate the expense.

Not to be deterred, the women in the WCTU sometimes paid the salaries of the matrons. And they argued

Frances Willard, president of the WCTU.
Library of Congress,
LC-DIG-ggbain-02864

that women could better handle other women without the use of force. (A newspaper reporter supported this idea by describing the way a matron would handle female prisoners: "A matron would invite her to walk into a sweet little cell and rest herself"—perhaps a bit of an exaggeration on the journalist's part!)

By the end of the 1800s most major cities and many smaller ones employed matrons. It was only the beginning of movements to put an end to the "outrageous state of things"—the lack of women jail matrons—as the *New York Times* saw it. And the appointment of matrons set the foundation for the next step—policewomen.

The hiring of matrons helped bring about an end to the treatment that female prisoners were subject to for over a century. As a reporter stated in the *Daily Globe* in St. Paul, Minnesota, those conditions were "an outrage on respectable civilization."

SADIE LIKENS

·················

Defying Denver's Powerful

HURDY-GURDY GIRLS, painted ladies, and saloon girls—
women who worked in dance halls went by a variety of names,
but most shared similar lives, in dangerous and oftentimes brutal surroundings. Late 1800s Colorado offered jobs for women
in the saloons and dance halls that peppered the landscape in
cow towns, mining camps, and cities across the state. Colorado
was part of what was called the Wild West; and while many
viewed it romantically, there was very little attractive about the
life of a saloon girl.

Not all were prostitutes, but it often became a slippery slope
resisting the plunge into the disreputable side of the saloon environment. Dance hall girls were paid to perform onstage, dance
with customers, and steer clients to the bar for more drinks.
The men paid about 50 cents for the privilege of dancing for 15
minutes with one of the girls, who earned a fraction of the fare.
It wasn't unusual for a woman to dance as many as 50 dances in
a night of drinking, gambling, and rabble-rousing.

A saloon in 1800s Colorado.
Library of Congress HABS COLO,8-STEL,8-1

It was through the ill-fated experiences of a young dance hall girl in Denver that Sadie Likens became the city's first police matron and advocate for the city's most vulnerable inhabitants.

It was sometime in 1886 that a young dance hall girl found herself pregnant and alone. She couldn't continue working, and she had nowhere to live. She had no one to turn to for help. Then she heard about the Woman's Christian Temperance Union (WCTU) and got in touch with women from the organization—one of whom contacted the young woman's family and told them about her situation. They were ashamed of their daughter and suggested she go to a reformatory. The young woman was heartbroken and desperate. And before the women of the WCTU could find a solution to her problem, she took her life.

WCTU: MORE THAN TEMPERANCE

••

"Agitate-Educate-Legislate." These were the watchwords of the WCTU. And through these actions women all over the United States brought about change.

A group of women determined to protest the dangers of alcohol, and later tobacco and other drugs, formed the organization in 1874 in Cleveland, Ohio. Chapters called "unions" then formed around the country.

Housewives and professional women marched— "the smaller ones in the front and the taller coming after"—to local saloons and drugstores that sold alcohol. When they arrived at their destinations they dropped to their knees to pray and sang their signature song, "Give to the Winds Thy Fears."

Eliminating the consumption of alcohol was not the WCTU's only cause. They agitated for reform in jails, prisons, and psychiatric ("insane") asylums. The WCTU members were appalled when they visited penal institutions to find women sometimes at the mercy of cruel men. They vowed to educate the public about the abuses they saw. In turn, they sought (and won) legislation—or at least action—on these fronts.

By 1890 the WCTU's efforts resulted in the hiring of matrons in 36 city jails, and chapters in 45 states were working for additional appointments. Portland (Maine), Denver, and Chicago all hired jail matrons after receiving pressure from the WCTU. In Portland the WCTU paid the matron's salary for the first year, until the city assumed the responsibility. In Buffalo,

New York, the WCTU was successful in getting the city to hire several matrons in 1885. And later the organization lobbied—successfully—for pay raises for the women.

The WCTU continues to advocate for causes today. They claim to be the "oldest voluntary, non-sectarian woman's organization in continuous existence in the world."

The experiences of the young dance hall woman spurred action from the WCTU members. The group had long fought the evils of alcohol and its adverse effects on families. They were also activists on behalf of destitute women and abused or neglected children, and 19th-century Colorado had plenty of both. Soon after the death of the young dance hall girl, the WCTU established the Colorado Cottage Home—a refuge for pregnant girls and women. And the organization chose one of their most energetic members—Sadie Likens—to run the new institute.

Sadie Likens.
Sam Howe Collection, Mss. 00199 (Scan #10027002), History Colorado, Denver, Colorado

Sadie had grappled with life's challenges herself by the time she became matron of Cottage Home. Her own mother had died when Sadie was only 4 years old. By the time she was 22 she had endured the death of her Union soldier husband and her firstborn child. Her second husband, William Likens, turned out to be a big disappointment. He also was a veteran of the Civil War and after the war became a lawyer. But his ethics were questionable. He was convicted of forgery and sentenced to four years of hard labor in the Colorado State Penitentiary. After serving most of his sentence, William was released and moved to Washington—without Sadie and their four children. By the time Sadie helped organize the Colorado Cottage Home, she was in need of a refuge herself. While she served as matron, she and her children lived at the home.

The Denver WCTU recognized another need in the city. In Denver, as in most cities, women who were arrested for various crimes were searched by male jailers and held in cells with male prisoners. Some of the women were prostitutes, and the men took advantage of them. Even women who were in jail for crimes such as shoplifting and drunkenness were not safe. Children who were runaways, lost, or whose parents had been arrested were also brought to the city jails. It was not a safe environment. The WCTU pressured the city to house women and children away from the male prisoners. And the organization wanted the city to hire a matron to protect and serve the female prisoners.

In 1888 the WCTU was successful in convincing the city to hire its first jail matron, and Sadie Likens got the job. Her duties were varied—looking after female prisoners, tending lost children, and questioning female witnesses. She was on call day and night to respond to the needs of the city jail. She tended sick and dying prisoners at all hours. Her job also required her to prevent crime and protect women and girls, which compelled her to enter dance halls, theaters, and houses of prostitution.

Some of Sadie's duties were frivolous and naturally fell to women working with men at the time. The unwritten rules stated that female employees cooked and served at the pleasure of the male officers. At the July Fourth celebration in 1891, Sadie, "a most genial of women," reportedly prepared an "elegant cold lunch" for the male officers. At the holiday season in 1895 Sadie was in charge of decorating the courtrooms with "American flags and evergreens." At the Christmas party she served "delicacies . . . for the pleasure of the boys in blue." However, Sadie was usually involved with much more serious obligations as Denver's police matron, such as overseeing custody of "two of the most notorious criminals ever captured in the West."

In 1892 Annie Watson (aka Queen of Shoplifters) and Tillie Williams engaged in "the most celebrated case of shoplifting in Denver." The case started when the two were arrested for stealing silk fabric from a store by concealing it under their clothing. Before the judge, they pleaded for leniency, as they had children at home who would suffer if they were detained. They were released, but not for long. A few days later police again arrested them for shoplifting. They were fined $25 and released. By this time authorities were suspicious of Tillie and Annie—suspecting they were entrenched in a grander burglary operation. Police obtained a search warrant for Tillie and Annie's house. As the police tried to gain entry Annie locked the door and began burning items in the stove—hoping to destroy evidence.

When the police got inside they discovered a treasure trove of goodies. The place was "stacked with stolen goods from cellar to attic." They discovered shipping receipts indicating big items had been stolen from local stores, sold, and shipped to cities across the country. This was no petty shoplifting scheme—it was a large-scale burglary ring. The women had been working in what police knew to be "the notorious Watson gang" consisting of the women, a man named Otto Reinche, and Jacob Watson (Tillie's husband).

It's unclear whether Sadie participated in the actual apprehension and investigation of the female gang members; however, she certainly encountered Tillie and Annie when they were taken into custody. While they were held in the jail where Sadie tended them, Tillie, Annie, and their children contracted scarlet fever. When it became apparent they needed hospitalization, the two saw the opportunity to make a getaway. As police were attempting to move them, Annie attacked Sadie, and Tillie tried to get Sadie's keys. A newspaper reported it took four men to subdue the two and place them back in their cells.

During the five years that Sadie served as matron, she was an extremely popular figure in Denver. Her "great and noble work" was well known around the city. And it was generally believed that "nobody could be found who could fill her place." At least that's what many of the citizens and Sadie's large circle of influential friends believed. But there were others who wanted to oust Sadie from her job for political reasons.

The city's police department was under the jurisdiction of a board comprised of men who Colorado governor Davis Waite appointed. The governor, who was a member of the Populist Party, wanted to ensure that people working in the police department were Populists as well, so he began to make that happen in May 1894.

Suddenly Sadie, who refused to declare allegiance to *any* political party, learned she was about to get two new employees in her department. One of the new employees, Kate Dwyer, happened to be a well-known Populist. Dwyer would be sharing Sadie's responsibilities as a *co*-matron. The second new employee would fill the role of assistant matron. Sadie was surprised that the police department could suddenly support *three* matrons!

For a couple of months Sadie continued to work with the two new employees, although she was unhappy about the situation. Then the board announced that to save money one of the matrons must go—and it was Sadie who would be terminated! Although the governor-appointed board initially said the reason was one of economy, others—including Kate Dwyer—began to circulate stories about Sadie's moral character.

Before Sadie had been fired, a friend—Ellen Harnett—placed an advertisement seeking work as a housekeeper in the *Rocky Mountain News*. Because Harnett did not have a permanent mailing address, she arranged to have responses sent to "Police Matron Likens at city hall." A man named Jesse Parr responded to the ad—sending it to the matron's office and addressing the letter to "Matron Likens."

When it arrived Sadie never saw the letter in which Parr admitted that he was tired of living alone in boardinghouses and provided a physical description of himself—"blue eyes, dark hair, smooth shaven face . . . a good friend to the right woman." Kate Dwyer got to it first, taking it to the police chief, the president of the police board, and eventually Governor Waite. Dwyer led the three men to believe that it was an indecent proposal from Parr to Sadie—and that Sadie had invited it. If it was true, it was certainly behavior unbecoming a police matron. But because it was likely these individuals were looking for any excuse to blemish Sadie's character, they never gave her the opportunity to explain.

When Sadie learned about the Parr letter, she decided she had to bring charges in order to save her reputation. "I would hardly have mixed myself up with the subject of this letter but

for the persistent manner in which friends kept telling me of a
certain letter . . . reflecting on my personal character," Sadie told
a reporter. Kate Dwyer, police board president Dennis Mullins,
police chief Hamilton Armstrong, and governor Davis Waite
were charged with interfering with the mail. They were taken
into custody and accused of being part of a conspiracy.

The governor was reportedly "boiling with indignation"
as he was "escorted" to the courthouse for arraignment.
The charges were read: "did conspire together to commit an
offense against the United States . . . did unlawfully take a letter
addressed . . . to Matron Likens . . . to obstruct the correspon-
dence . . . and pry into the business and secrets of Mrs. Likens
. . . and did embezzle the same."

But before the week was up the charges against Governor
Waite were dropped. No one could prove that he had actually seen Parr's letter. Within a very short time the conspiracy
charges against all involved were dropped when prosecutors
determined there was not enough evidence. But the public created such an uproar that Sadie was reinstated as matron when
the Populist Party lost in the next elections.

Sadie eventually resigned from her matron position to
become superintendent of the State Home and Industrial School
for Girls. Throughout the rest of her career she headed up a
variety of social agencies in Denver while also raising her four
children. In addition to helping needy women and children, she
worked on behalf of Civil War and World War I veterans. She
died in 1920. A monument honoring her stands near the Colorado state capitol.

The actions of a desolate dance hall girl—whose name has
long been forgotten—went unnoticed by many in an unforgiving and intolerant society in 1880s Colorado. But the women of
the WCTU took notice and were moved to help other defense-

less young women. They supported social agencies that gave refuge to homeless and abused women and children. They put pressure on the city police department to hire a matron to protect women and children who entered the jail system. The nameless dance hall girl who faced utter despair inspired others to offer comfort and hope. Sadie Likens was one of those who noticed and took action.

LEARN MORE

"Sadie Likens: Patron of the Fallen" by Annette L. Student, *Colorado Heritage*, summer 2001

Tales, Trails and Tommyknockers: Stories from Colorado's Past by Myriam Friggens (Johnson Books, 2012)

Woman's Christian Temperance Union
www.wctu.org/index.html

ALETHA GILBERT

....

City Mother

TEENAGE GIRLS IN Los Angeles in 1915 who attended wild parties in "immoral places," danced the highly "suggestive" shimmy or bunny hop in dance halls, or lost their inhibitions through the consumption of liquor ran the risk of running into their mother. Not their *real* mother—the *"city* mother," Aletha Gilbert.

The City Mother's Bureau was only a year old, having been established at the suggestion of Aletha Gilbert, a policewoman from the juvenile bureau of the Los Angeles Police Department. She planned to intervene in cases where "wayward boys and girls" were in danger of engaging in more serious acts that would land them in the courts.

With an annual budget of $400, Aletha headed up the new bureau. A group of 11 prominent women in the Los Angeles area—wealthy society ladies and social workers—aided her. They were sometimes referred to as the Golden Rule Squad but usually simply as the City Mother's Bureau. The committee

Aletha Gilbert (fifth from the left) and Lucy Thompson Gray (sixth from left) with the Los Angeles Police Department.
James A. Bultema, Guardians of Angels: A History of the Los Angeles Police Department

members served on a volunteer basis and were primarily in an advisory role, although they did have police badges. Aletha was the only city mother earning a salary.

"Keeping children out of court will be our endeavor," Aletha explained. Both boys and girls were brought to the offices of the city mother, where she gave them a "good talking to in a motherly way." As the city's youths showed up at Aletha's doorstep, she investigated their home situations; and where these were found to be "defective," she counseled parents.

The bureau offices were located in an old school building far removed from the regular police headquarters to prevent youths intermingling with hardened criminals. In addition, the new bureau kept client cases confidential and out of the press whenever possible.

While the bureau helped both boys and girls, there was an emphasis on helping girls and women. Some cases involved unmanageable girls whose desperate mothers brought them to the bureau. Other times girls came to the city mother from abusive homes or from situations where the mother and daughter simply couldn't get along.

"While I talk to many girls who have become unmanageable and are in danger from the evils of the city, I also have to advise unwise mothers," Aletha said.

Aletha's life in police work began long before she convinced her chief of police to set up the new bureau. She joined the Los Angeles Police Department in 1902 as an assistant to her mother, Lucy Thompson Gray, the city's first police matron (hired in 1888). When Lucy died in 1904, Aletha stepped into her position.

By that time Aletha was a single mother of a daughter. There are different versions of her status. She was either a divorcée or a widow. Historian and author Janis Appier found evidence of a marriage at age 16 and a divorce at 27; however, Aletha referred to herself as a widow.

As matron, Aletha worked 12-hour shifts caring for all the female prisoners who entered police custody. There were always at least a few women in the city's jails. Some were serving sentences; others were awaiting trial. The matron was responsible for the safety and health of the prisoners. Aletha looked after the meals for the female inmates, took them to the hospital when they were seriously ill, and directed their work while in jail. She tried to "lighten their burden of sorrow" by bringing them books and decorative needlework to keep them in a "cheerful frame of mind." All these duties earned Aletha a $75-per-month salary.

MARY JENKS: BEHIND THE BARS

· ·

"Mamma, I have brought you some tomatoes, there was nothing else in the house to eat."

Eight-year-old Katie was visiting her mother and father in the Pawtucket, Rhode Island, city jail, where matron Mary Jenks recorded the exchange between mother and child in her 1902 book *Behind the Bars, or Ten Years of the Life of a Police Matron*.

But Katie's mother was not impressed with her little girl's efforts. She ordered Katie to travel by foot to a town two miles away to ask an aunt for money to secure release of the parents. Almost five hours later, Katie returned—tired, hungry, and "melted."

As Mary described it, the mother called her daughter "hard names" and threatened "to break every bone in her body" if she didn't find the money somewhere. And, the mother warned, Katie had better do it quickly, or she "would pull every hair off her head."

Later, returning yet again without money, Katie begged the matron to break the news to her mother. When she did, the woman "flew into a passion, accused the child of lying and threatened everything horrid and inhuman."

Finally Mary convinced the police chief to release the jailed mother without paying the fines.

This is one of the numerous stories Mary Jenks included in her book. The City of Pawtucket hired her in 1893 at the urging of the local Woman's Christian Temperance Union (WCTU) despite the dire prediction by the chief of police that the work of a jail matron "was so degrading and revolting that no pure-minded, respectable woman would take it."

Aletha's years as police matron gave her insight into the justice system as it applied to female prisoners. She became an advocate for the women she saw pass through her jail. One area of concern was the lack of educational opportunities the women faced. And she decided to do something about it.

"If we can teach one woman in 10 something that will help to make her life easier and better when she leaves it will be sufficient," Aletha asserted in the spring of 1910 as she talked about the school she was starting for the 20 women who were incarcerated in the Los Angeles jail. For many it was the first time in their lives they would attend school. The curriculum consisted of domestic science—cooking, sewing, housekeeping—and even a training school for nurses.

A jail school.
Library of Congress, LC-DIG-NPCC-28432

Aletha also blamed women's low wages and lack of work skills as reasons for many turning to crime. "About two-thirds [of the women in the jails] found they could not make enough money to live honestly. They lost heart and began to slip. It is sad, but this is the best place most of them have to go."

She put the female inmates to work preparing their own food, doing laundry and ironing for themselves and the jail staff, and mending linens. "To shut women up without an effort to make them better is useless and cruel," Aletha said.

Whenever the Los Angeles police had to deal with children, they assigned Aletha to the case. So in the fall of 1910 it was not surprising to see the matron in court testifying in a child custody case that would decide the fate of a seven-month-old baby who had been taken in by a couple hoping to adopt him. When Aletha entered the case, the only thing she knew with certainty was that someone would end up with a broken heart.

Aletha first joined the case when a woman named Helen Whiting was arrested for stealing from the store where she worked. While in jail, she told Aletha her unusual story.

She had given birth to a baby boy seven months before being arrested. For some reason—perhaps because she was not yet married to the baby's father—while she was under the influence of chloroform immediately after the baby's birth, her parents forced her to sign a paper, which she learned later meant she had given up all rights to the baby. From that day forward Helen said she had longed for her baby boy and began to search for him. At some point she had married the baby's father, Homer Whiting, and together they searched for their child.

Meanwhile Helen took a job in a department store and began stealing small baby articles that she hoped to use with her baby when she found him. When Aletha told the sentencing judge at the hearing all of this, he gave Helen probation.

But it wasn't the end of the story. Aletha appealed to a woman's club to help with Helen and Homer Whiting's plight. The club formed a committee to help find the child. And under Aletha's direction, the women traced the baby to the Los Angeles Home-Finding Society for Children. There they learned the baby was living with foster parents, who had been told they could adopt him after a year.

In the end the biological parents and the foster parents had to take their custody battle to court. The atmosphere in the courtroom was extremely "hostile" as the hearing unfolded. The turning point occurred when Helen saw her baby for the first time. There wasn't a dry eye in the courtroom as she clasped the "fat, blue-eyed infant in her arms and cooed and cried over" him. The judge ruled in favor of the biological parents. Even the foster parents agreed that the natural parents deserved the baby.

Despite such success stories, by the time Aletha had been working as a police matron for 10 years, she was feeling some frustration with her job. One especially troubling aspect was that she did not have arrest powers. When she saw a crime being committed, she had to call in a police officer—always a male—to make the actual arrest. In August 1910 the City of Los Angeles hired its first female police officer—a woman named Alice Stebbins Wells. It's possible Aletha became a little jealous and also wanted to become an actual officer.

She made the request in 1911 and in 1912 was upgraded to police officer and assigned to the juvenile bureau, where she handled cases involving young girls, women under age 21, and boys under age 8. In addition, she investigated crimes involving female suspects, witnesses, and victims of any age. It was her duty to inspect public places of amusement for signs of "immorality and crime." And she escorted to their homes girls in public places whom she felt were in danger of being injured physically or corrupted morally.

Sixteen-year-old Lulu Breger was one of the girls who Aletha saved from "moral corruption." In the fall of 1912 Lulu left her home in Pennsylvania to marry a Los Angeles man named Percy Van Horn. The girl's father knew she was headed to Los Angeles, and provided the police with her description, hoping they would locate the runaway teen.

Aletha happened to be riding a streetcar one day when she spotted a girl matching Lulu's description in a group of pedestrians. The car was moving far too fast for the policewoman to jump off and question her. The next day officers began searching boardinghouses in the neighborhood where Aletha had seen the girl. Soon they apprehended Lulu and took her to the city jail, where she admitted to Aletha that she intended to marry Percy Van Horn. But the marriage was not to happen, as the teenager was held by police until her dad could come from Pennsylvania.

After only two years in the juvenile bureau, Aletha recognized the need for an alternative to juvenile court for the young people she encountered. She believed young offenders deserved a second chance and that the *threat* of court was more powerful than an actual conviction. She turned her attentions to establishing the City Mother's Bureau—allowing her to devote her time to *preventing* crime rather than *investigating* crimes. She presented the concept to her chief of police, and he obtained the approval of the city council and mayor. City officials decided Aletha would head up the new bureau, which would handle cases confidentially and without publicity.

"I was constantly meeting with young boys and girls who had taken a slight misstep . . . who needed a little kindly advice . . . rather than punishment," Aletha explained about her desire for a city mother's bureau. "I began to realize that real mothers who would and could let their light shine outside as well as inside their homes were one of the greatest needs in stemming the tide of youthful folly," she added.

As individuals entered the office of City Mother Gilbert, they were greeted by a "kind-faced, motherly woman" with "soft gray hair" and "eyes [that] are kind and blue." However, if the sight of the caring woman lulled girls into thinking they were about to embark on a pleasant visit with their grandmother, they might be mistaken. A newspaper reporter wrote, "For all her kindly matronliness, Mrs. Gilbert has a shrewd way of going to the roots of difficulties and righting them from the ground up."

Certainly Lola Gonzales, who Aletha arrested after she tried to escape arrest through a window, saw little in the way of softness in the city mother's demeanor. The young woman was dancing in a preview show at a motion picture theater when the cord holding her costume's breast plate in place broke. The broken cord may have been out of her control; however, Lola continued to dance without her costume, and that got her arrested.

In 1915 the City of Los Angeles was dealing with another problem that at first glance appeared fairly innocent; however, the "pennant stands" that had popped up on street corners were far from harmless. They were actually fronts for prostitution. Young women worked at booths displaying a variety of sports team pennants. They were intended to attract passing men, who rolled dice for a pennant. But the stands were actually intended to lure men in so the women could arrange rendezvous later. City Mother Gilbert and her voluntary committee of city mothers, armed only with their badges, were successful in putting the pennant stands out of business.

As city mother, Aletha was called in to handle an unusual case in September 1915. It's unclear what caused the police to investigate Professor Eugene de Forest, who operated a school for the dramatic arts, but it was the city mother who arrested and charged the professor with "masquerading as a man."

"I was born a girl, with the soul of a man," explained Eugene when he was arrested by Aletha. He admitted he had been living as a man for 25 years and had been married twice—early in his life to a man and later to a woman. As an actor, Eugene had played male roles without detection.

"When City Mother Gilbert arrested me I was dumbfounded, but knew my duplicity had been discovered," Eugene said. However, he concluded, "I have wronged no one." In the end the police agreed and released Eugene without bringing formal charges against him.

Los Angeles's role in the motion picture industry brought riches to many in the early 1920s, but it brought headaches to the City Mother's Bureau. Many young people were drawn to the glitz and glamour of the movies. They came from all parts of the country to get their big break in the movies.

Many of the girls who were "afflicted with the silver screen bacillus [literally, 'bacteria,' or bug]" ended up in Aletha's office—broke, frightened, and desperate. It fell to the city mother to help them get "real jobs" so they could earn railroad fare home.

Over the years the role of the city mother expanded. The focus continued to be girls and young women; however, the bureau helped boys and men too. And the bureau became a type of domestic relations court as well.

In 1915 a teenage boy named Charles Fulmer caught the attention of Aletha and the City Mother's Bureau. He was the son of a single mother, who was "absent" from his life. He had put himself through high school by doing janitorial work and graduated with exceptional grades and high praise from his teachers. Charles wanted to attend college and hoped to study medicine. However, he was in need of a summer job so he could earn enough money to enroll in college in the fall. The City Mother's Bureau made an appeal to the public for someone to hire the boy for the summer.

It was not unusual for husbands and wives to appeal to the city mother for help when they were experiencing difficulties in their relationships. She always offered her services freely and confidentially, so she and her fellow policewomen "soothed and solved" "domestic troubles of all kinds." In addition to wives who were "neglected by their husbands," husbands who held "grievances" against their wives sought the city mother's advice.

It was because of Aletha's boundless desire to reach out to men, women, and children; her simple motherly advice; and her advocacy for Los Angeles's most vulnerable that her reputation was well known in all parts of the city as well as across the country. In 1929, close to the end of her career as city mother, a popular author wrote this about Aletha's work: "While orange groves, prune trees, oil wells, and gold may be the advertised bounties of California, Aletha Gilbert is making a corner of the great state beautiful through deeds of courage and kindness."

LEARN MORE

Behind the Bars, or Ten Years of the Life of a Police Matron by Mary Jenks (Pawtucket, RI, 1902)

Guardians of Angels: A History of the Los Angeles Police Department by James A. Bultema (Infinity, 2013)

PART II

"COPETTES" NO LONGER

Policewomen

A DETROIT POLICEWOMAN was patrolling the streets of her district late one night in 1933 when she came across a tiny girl selling candy and paper flowers on a street corner. The girl appeared undernourished and sickly. The policewoman learned the girl, Eleanor, was 11 years old and attended school infrequently because she didn't have proper clothes to wear. Eleanor, who lived with her dad, stepmother, and two siblings, was forced to work the street selling and begging. It was a typical scene for many policewomen in the early 1900s.

It's difficult to put a precise starting point on an era. When were women in law enforcement finally taken seriously enough to warrant official titles—away from copettes, guardettes, and police in petticoats? When was the first policewoman hired? When was the term *policewoman* first used? Some of the women who were called copettes or matrons were actually doing the work of police officers. Many of the matrons' positions evolved

Policewoman practicing self-defense.
Library of Congress, LC-USZ62-116716

into policewoman positions. So it's a very murky undertaking to try to pin dates on firsts.

Some of the first who were labeled policewomen included Florence Klotz, in Allegheny, Pennsylvania, (a "constable in petticoats") in 1897; Helen Wilder, a Hawaiian police officer, in

1899; and Mary Owens, in Chicago in 1901. Others include Portland, Oregon's Lola G. Baldwin in 1908 and Alice Stebbins Wells in Los Angeles in 1910.

Regardless of who was first, early policewomen shared common attributes and experiences. They became policewomen after considerable agitation by outside groups or through their own dogged initiative. They were treated differently from their male counterparts; their duties were tightly prescribed; and they couldn't advance to higher positions within the system. Sometimes they worked in segregated departments called women's bureaus. They almost all had to overcome sexism in their workplaces.

In the early 1900s, as more and more cities hired policewomen, their responsibilities were clearly defined—limited to dealing with women and children. The trend was toward using policewomen as social workers. They were protectors and charged with prevention of crime. Their beats were stores, parks, depots, and amusement parks. They were responsible for previewing the latest movies and informing theater managers of indecent performances. Any sex crimes were considered the concern of policewomen. They prepared police cases for court and accompanied their charges to court appearances. During wartimes they were responsible for protecting the nation's soldiers at training camps across the country from prostitutes and saving innocent girls from lonely soldiers. And they *were* women, the thinking went—so any housekeeping and social event planning fell to the policewomen.

Policewomen had a heavy load in almost any city in the land! It was a title that held a great deal of responsibility, but it was a sexist term that limited women's duties and careers. It wasn't until the 1970s that the distinction between male and female police officers was finally eliminated.

ISABELLA GOODWIN

····················

Saving Face

IT WAS AN "IMPENETRABLE mystery" that had baffled the New York City Police Department for weeks. In 1912 two messengers from the East River National Bank had been robbed of $25,000. The victims had been beat senseless. It was a tale that gripped the country, according to a *New York Times* article at the time. And the police were unable to solve the crime. In the end it took the detective skills of a woman named Isabella Goodwin to "save the face" of the police department.

Isabella was born in 1865 in Greenwich Village. As a young woman she married John W. Goodwin, a police officer. In 1895, when Isabella was 30 years old, John died, leaving her to support their four children. She decided she wanted to work for the New York City Police Department as her husband had. It was not unusual in those days for police departments to give jobs to widows of officers. However, Isabella was not handed the job merely because her husband had been a policeman. She studied and passed an exam; and in May 1896 she was hired.

For a few years Isabella performed the duties of a typical police matron. She looked out for the welfare of women who were brought into the station for a variety of reasons. She made sure the women were kept separate from the male prisoners and were treated well by male officers. She kept an eye on female prisoners who were suicide risks and found shelter for children whose mothers were in jail.

After Isabella had been working as a matron for about six years, something happened that became a turning point in her life. The captain needed a woman to go undercover to capture some people who were running an illegal gambling establishment—betting on the horse races. The business was operating in a poolroom that was open only to women patrons. The police suspected the illegal activities were taking place there, but they needed proof. They needed a woman to get into the poolroom and gather evidence. The captain asked Isabella to help out.

Isabella went undercover to see what she could learn. She spent time in the neighborhood where the poolroom was located. She made it known that she was interested in gambling, and soon she met a woman who took her into the pool hall. "What do you know about horses?" one of the women running the place asked her.

"Sleepyhead looks good to me," Isabella responded. And she placed a $5 bet on a horse named Sleepyhead.

Within a short time Isabella had gathered evidence to bring charges against the women. But because she was only a matron, she did not have arrest powers. She gave the information to the male officers, and they lost no time in raiding the poolroom.

"My, I never saw such excitement in my life when I heard the police battering down the doors," Isabella recalled. The women began to scream and "run around like hens without their

GREENWICH VILLAGE: "THE VILLAGE"

It started as a marshy swamp called Sapokanican by Native Americans in the 18th century. And for years it was cleared and cultivated as farmland. Some of its farmers included African Americans who were former slaves. The city's homeless were buried in a potter's field there, and the city gallows were situated in Greenwich Village in the 1780s (present-day Washington Square Park).

By the time Isabella Goodwin was born (1865) in the area of New York City known as Greenwich Village, the makeup of the neighborhood had changed. Bordered on the north by West 14th Street, Houston Street on the south, the Hudson River on the west, and Broadway on the east, the district had undergone several transitions. Commercial enterprises had grown up along the river's edge, where housewives could buy fresh produce at the open-air markets. Neat row houses held middle-class merchants and tradesmen and their families. More prosperous families settled around Washington Square Park after the city closed the potter's field. The neighborhood had become a center for art and literature.

Waves of French, Irish, and Italian immigrants moved into the Village in the late 19th century. And as they moved in, the more fashionable residents moved out—to the Fifth Avenue and Central Park areas. Breweries, warehouses, coal and lumber yards, and large factories—including the infamous Triangle Shirtwaist Factory—set up business and provided jobs for the newly arrived immigrants. Multifamily tenements housed the workers.

By the end of World War I in 1919 another transition was taking place. The Village was becoming a mecca for artists, writers, poets, musicians, and actors. And that movement continued into the 1930s, '40s, '50s, '60s, and '70s. Many colorful and creative individuals took up residency, built businesses, established offices, and launched movements from Greenwich Village. Today the area that was once called Sapokanican continues to be a coveted neighborhood that draws tourists and native New Yorkers alike.

Drawing depicting fashionable woman in Greenwich Village in the 1830s.
Library of Congress, LC-USZ62-87654

heads," she later described the scene. "Those gambling ladies really hadn't a drop of sporting blood left."

The arresting officers rounded up the women and loaded them into the patrol wagon for a ride to the station. Isabella never blew her cover, managing to slip away from the wagon before it headed to the station. Since the gambling women never knew Isabella had been working with the police, she was free to participate in future undercover assignments.

Isabella's poolroom assignment showed her supervisors that she could be valuable to them in investigative work. She was

Illustration from 1913 making a joke about a policewoman's indecision about working or shopping.
Library of Congress, LC-DIG-ppmsca-27937

ready to do more, and they were willing to give her additional opportunities. Her appearance often worked to her advantage. She was described as "attractive and gracious." Her "bright brown eyes" and "quiet friendliness of manner" were her best disguises. Criminals didn't expect a woman, especially one who looked like Isabella—"middle aged and respectable looking"— to be anything other than a cultivated society lady.

Her new job duties led her down some interesting paths. And she met some unique individuals on the streets of New York City. In the early 1900s the city was teeming with fortune-tellers, clairvoyants, and bogus doctors—scammers who were happy to take money from gullible people. Their activities were illegal, and the police were kept busy enforcing the laws.

Over the next nine years Isabella spent most of her working hours gathering evidence, arresting (always along with a "real" police officer—a man), and testifying in court. She usually worked in clandestine operations and often dressed in disguise. There was the time Isabella went undercover to investigate a woman who claimed she had healing powers.

"She told me to turn my back to her, took my hands and told me to relax," Isabella explained.

The woman pressed her hand against Isabella's forehead and said, "Now I will enter into your consciousness and you will be cured." She proclaimed Isabella cured and charged her $2. Isabella asked the woman if she was a hypnotist. She replied that she was a "suggestionist." Because of Isabella's work, the woman was charged with practicing medicine without a license.

Then there was the time Isabella saw a sign displayed in a window: DEMONSTRATOR OF IMMORTALITY. It caught her attention, and she decided to investigate. Upon entering the building, she was met by a woman. Isabella said she wanted to have contact with her dead sister. The woman charged her 50 cents and led her into a room with black curtains covering the windows. In a few minutes a white figure appeared and began to moan, "Sister, my dear sister!"

"Are you happy?" Isabella asked.

As the figure began to glide away, Isabella jumped up, grabbed the "ghost," and dragged it to the window, where she drew the curtains aside and pulled the sheet from the figure. It was a "pretty little blonde girl" whom Isabella knew to be the daughter of the "demonstrator."

And she never forgot the man posing as a medical doctor who diagnosed her with a malignant cancer brought about by "overindulgence in cream soda." Of course, he was eager to sell her medicine that would cure her ailment.

More than one fortune-teller foresaw a man in Isabella's life. Adeline Herman, "one of New York's best known seeresses," dispensed advice to Isabella when she posed as a client. "If thou wouldst catch a hubby, oh young girl of uncertain years, study the way of the widow. They know how to cop the men. Be a little forward." Her advice earned her a night in jail with bail set at $500.

"All of them assumed I wanted a husband," Isabella said about the fortune-tellers she encountered, "which I didn't!"

She worked long hours, and sometimes when she went undercover she didn't get home to see her children—who were cared for by her mother—for days. "Sometimes it's pretty hard work. I have had 14 cases in the night court in a single night—with 14 different lawyers trying to rattle me and distort my testimony," she said.

Isabella met with great success as a New York City Police Department matron. Although she was performing the duties of a police *detective*, she did not hold the title, receive the salary, or earn the recognition that her male counterparts did. That all changed early in 1912 when a gang of criminals known as the Taxi Cab Robbers became the most wanted men in New York City and had the misfortune of meeting up with Isabella Goodwin.

Every week Wilbur Smith and Frank Wardle, employees of the East River National Bank, took a cab to the Produce Exchange National Bank. Each week they carried large sums of money between the two financial institutions. The amount of the transfer varied, but on February 15, 1912, they had bundles of bills valued at $25,000. As the cab wove its way through the city streets, it slowed to a crawl. Suddenly a man stumbled into the path of the cab, and it came to a stop. Immediately the rear doors of the vehicle were opened, and two men lunged into the backseat. They started to beat and punch Wilbur and Frank. At the same time, a third man opened the front passenger door and hopped into the cab. The driver was forced to take the three hoodlums to an elevated train, and that was the last anyone saw of them or the money.

The police commissioner assigned 60 of his detectives to the case. For days the New York Police Department followed leads and questioned witnesses—including the cab driver, Geno Mantani. Police identified the suspects as Gene Splaine ("the Parrot"), Billy Keller ("Dutch"), and Eddie Kinsman ("Eddie the Boob"). They also learned about Eddie's sweetheart, Annie Hull ("Swede Annie").

Days went by with no arrests, and the citizens of New York began to question the abilities of the police. A newspaper account described the entire department as "the subject of jest and cartoon from coast to coast." It wasn't a reputation the police commissioner wanted to maintain.

When police detectives heard that Swede Annie was living in a boardinghouse in the city, they decided to use Isabella as a "roper"—someone who helped get suspected criminals into the police net. She got a job as a cleaning lady where Swede Annie and a friend were living. By listening carefully at doors and engaging the two in conversations, Isabella learned much about the whereabouts of the robbers.

One day Swede Annie came back after an out-of-town trip. She looked quite glamourous in a new hat and suit. Isabella overheard Swede Annie tell her friend, "Well, Eddie the Boob turned the trick all right." Isabella learned that Eddie had purchased Annie's new clothes in a store in Albany. She got the name of the store owner and passed it on to the police commissioner. The clothier confirmed that a man of Eddie's description had bought the clothes and was "shedding money like a canary does feathers in the molting season."

Most important, Isabella discovered that Eddie was back in New York City—but not for long. He and Swede Annie were planning to leave for San Francisco the following day. This was all the detectives needed to make their arrests at Grand Central Station as the two were buying tickets.

There was little honor among the thieves, and each ratted on the other. Others were also implicated—including the cabbie and the man who ran into the path of the cab. The taxicab bandits were eventually tried and convicted.

When Isabella recalled her role in the events, she admitted, "My flesh creeps sometimes—for these robbers were desperate men. I guess my life wouldn't have been worth much if they had suspected."

The day after the arrests, Isabella was called into the police commissioner's office. He informed her that he was promoting her to detective! Isabella's new position meant her salary would more than double—from $1,000 to $2,250 per year. Newspapers across the country reported on her status as the "first municipal woman detective in the world." (In reality she was certainly the first municipal woman detective in New York City, but not in the world. Others preceded her.)

Isabella was unimpressed with her newfound fame. "I do not care for the distinction of being the first woman to become a member of the detective force. But I hope my work will be so successful that I will be known as one of the cleverest detectives in the department," she told a newspaper reporter. "I love the excitement and I want to show just what a woman can do when the chance comes her way."

Isabella continued to make a name for herself. None of her subsequent work gained as much attention as the taxicab robbery, but her name appeared frequently in news reports. When the Metropolitan Opera wanted to discourage speculators (or scalpers, as they would be known today), they sought help from the police department. At a performance of the opera *Carmen*, Isabella and fellow officers strolled in front of the Met dressed in finery and "looking anxiously about them at the throng waiting for standing room." In time they were approached by speculators who offered them tickets at inflated prices. They nabbed five culprits in one night.

When a gangster was on trial for the murder of a New York City police officer, no one would testify against him. One by one, witnesses whom the state had lined up for testimony changed their stories. Suddenly no one had seen anything. There was one exception. Sixteen-year-old Nellie di Carlo told police what she had seen from the window of her home. To keep her safe before her court appearance, she was put under the protection of Isabella, who "kept her from any influences" that would prevent her testimony.

In another case a crowd attacked Isabella and a fellow detective when they attempted to arrest a "gypsy princess." Maria Marandi was a popular fortune-teller, and her fans resented the police's interruption of her services. Armed with a warrant, Isabella was "much disheveled" as she made her way back to the police station with the princess in her grip.

For Isabella life as a detective was not much different from work as a matron. Certainly the salary was better. She did not wear a uniform or carry a gun, as the men did. She continued to handle many of the duties she had before becoming a detective. However, in addition to making more money, Isabella received recognition and credit for the dangerous, vital work she did to serve and protect the citizens of New York City.

In 1921 Isabella had earned the rank of lieutenant, and she and another officer, Mary Hamilton, were assigned to head up the newly formed women's bureau of the police department. It was a separate division consisting of 26 female officers. They were responsible for dealing with juveniles, runaways, truants, and young girls and women who arrived in the city with no money or place to stay. They supervised amusement parks, dance halls, and other recreation facilities.

Another memorable event occurred in Isabella's life in 1921, and it had nothing to do with her work as a detective. "I consider it a personal matter and don't intend to say anything about it. Why should anyone care whether I have married or not?" And that's all she would tell a reporter for the *Evening World* on November 28.

Fifty-six-year-old Isabella broke all sorts of social norms when she married Oscar Seaholm, a man 30 years her junior, in 1921. In a time when few women pursued careers—especially after marriage and having children—Isabella continued to work as a detective. She also chose to keep her name rather than using her husband's—very rare in those days.

Breaking barriers had long been part of Isabella's life. When she began as a matron in the late 1890s, she was one of a handful of women working at the police department. She took the job because she was a widow with children and needed the income. However, it became more than just a job.

"I threw myself body and soul into the work," Isabella reminisced about her early days on the force. "I think I was born for just such work. . . . The excitement always keeps one's interest at the fever point."

Isabella added, "It's not a career that I would recommend to every woman. But it is a lot better than those of the majority of women I know. And there is the added incentive of knowing that you are doing something really worthwhile."

By the time she retired, Isabella had served 30 years with the New York City Police Department. Her profession was a good fit for this "small figure" of a woman with a "kind, motherly face." She helped serve and protect generations of New York City citizens. Isabella claimed to have benefited from her years of service too: "The things I have learned about poor, weak human nature! My experiences would fill a book."

LEARN MORE

The Fearless Mrs. Goodwin: How New York's First Female Detective Cracked the Crime of the Century by Elizabeth Mitchell (Byliner, 2011)

The Greenwich Village Society for Historic Preservation
www.gvshp.org/_gvshp/resources/history.htm

"Isabella Goodwin" search at Chronicling America
http://chroniclingamerica.loc.gov

Policewomen: A History, 2nd ed., by Kerry Segrave (McFarland, 2014)

GRACE WILSON

·················

Breaking Color Lines

"THERE IS ONE BLANKET that is thick with lice. The place stinks."

Anna, a young "colored girl," was spending time in Chicago's Harrison Street Jail for a petty crime she may or may not have committed. She reminded herself that the nation's justice system considered her innocent until proven guilty, but she felt as though she was being punished. She was awaiting a court date.

When the lice weren't bothering Anna, the bed bugs nearly drove her mad. When she was first placed in the cell it was "full of cigarette stubs and glutinous gobs of spit that made me sick to look at."

The jailers gave Anna and the other female prisoners few considerations. There was no privacy. "When we change clothes we have to do it in the open and the policemen watch with guffaws and jibes. The whole thing is absolutely indecent as well as uncomfortable," she said.

"The officers are always looking the women prisoners over, talking about the girls' legs and making out-of-place remarks," Anna said. "The toilet is in the hall and is not protected from sight of men who are ungentlemanly enough to want to watch, poke fun, and say nasty things."

"When I was first put in I was placed in a cell with 16 others. There was not even room to lie down on the floor. We had to stand up all night."

It was 1915, and Anna's situation was not unusual for women hauled into jail on suspicion of crimes. Chicago was not unlike other cities. Being a woman under arrest could be an extremely degrading experience. However, it could be less traumatic when policewomen—rather than men—were making the arrests. But there weren't always policewomen at every jail in the city. Some—such as the one where Anna was held—had only male police officers.

More than 20 years before Anna's experience, the Chicago Police Department hired their first policewoman. She was a white woman named Marie Owens. Over the years additional women were hired as police officers. But it took much longer for the city to hire its first African American policewoman, Grace Wilson.

During the early 1900s Chicago's African American population grew rapidly as hundreds of thousands chose to leave the South, where they faced discrimination and hard economic times. This mass movement of people north and west to urban areas became known as the Great Migration. By 1919 roughly 100,000 African Americans had established homes in Chicago, up from about 44,000 in 1909.

African Americans soon began to question the lack of representation in city agencies—especially on the police force.

SHE HAD SEEN ALL THERE WAS TO SEE

Policewoman Georgia Hill Robinson was scouring the city of Los Angeles looking for the kidnapper of a 12-year-old girl when she received word that the little girl's body had been found. It was badly mutilated, and it was a sight Georgia would never forget.

Georgia was the first African American policewoman in Los Angeles—and by some accounts the first in the country. She began working for the police department in 1916, first as a volunteer matron. By 1919 she was a policewoman handling primarily juvenile and homicide cases involving African American offenders. She became so renowned that she was the first person mothers of "unmanageable" daughters turned to for help.

"My great aim is to insist on girls getting an equal break with men in delinquency cases," Georgia said.

Georgia Hill Robinson.
Los Angeles Public Library

This French-speaking, self-educated woman had earned a reputation as an activist in civil and political circles in Leadville, Colorado, before moving to Los Angeles, where she became known as "the female Booker T. Washington" of the city.

Georgia retired from police work in 1928 after being blinded in an incident with an offender. The injury did not keep her from continuing her volunteer work in the community, however.

"I didn't need my eyes any longer. I had seen all there was to see," Georgia remarked in an interview with *Ebony* magazine in 1954.

Women's clubs, the *Chicago Defender* newspaper, and community leaders put pressure on the city's officials—asking for representation of black women in the police. After years of petitioning, finally in March 1918 the city hired an African American woman as a policewoman!

"Who are *you*? You don't look good to me," sneered a white attorney outside a Chicago courtroom. He was speaking to Grace Wilson as she stood by the side of a defendant in the hall near a stairwell.

"I am a police officer, and if you don't go on down those stairs I'll put you in a cell that may look better," Grace replied.

Some described her as a woman of "culture and refinement," and she certainly didn't deserve the contempt shown by the attorney. Grace was a graduate of Evansville High School, Indiana, and had completed special training at the School of Civics and Philanthropy (which became part of the University of Chicago's School of Social Service Administration). She was working as a house mother at the Illinois State Training School for Delinquent Girls in Geneva, Illinois (later called the Illinois State Training School for Girls), when black community leaders encouraged her to take the civil service examination for police work. Grace passed with high scores and was hired on March 28, 1918, as Chicago's first African American policewoman, at a salary of $1,000 per year.

POLICEWOMAN MAKES TEN ARRESTS read the headline in a Chicago newspaper soon after Grace's hire. She had been a busy police officer during her first weeks on the job. However, her duties probably weren't what she thought they would be when she decided to apply for the position.

The world was in the grips of the great influenza epidemic. The Chicago health commissioner had launched a campaign to curb the spread of the disease, and the city had banned spitting in public areas. The police took their duties seriously, and Grace was most vigilant. Her first 10 arrests were for spitters! Her diligence did not go unnoticed by her commanding officer, who "highly complimented" Grace for her work.

While Grace contributed a valuable service to the police department in her roundup of spitters, she soon turned to more serious and dangerous activities. In May two men got into a fight over 25 cents during a gambling event, and one of the men plunged a knife into the abdomen of the other. The four-inch-long, eight-inch-deep cut caused the death of the victim. The suspect got away before police arrived at the scene of the crime.

Within a week Grace and a fellow policeman had tracked down the suspect in a fashionable apartment building near Lake Michigan. After the arrest, Grace's commanding officer again commended her "efficient work" in the capture of the criminal, and he recognized her as the first policewoman in the history of the department to capture a murder suspect.

Later that summer Grace and another male police officer tried to break up a fight between two men armed with knives. The two were fighting over a woman, who also became involved in the melee. One of the men was seriously wounded by the time officers were able to subdue the participants. As the policeman left to call a patrol wagon, the woman attempted to strike Grace with a whisky flask she had concealed in her clothes. According to a newspaper report, the woman dropped the bottle when she "looked down the lonesome road of the policewoman's gun barrel."

Over the next few years Grace made a name for herself, usually handling female suspects and juveniles but also occasionally becoming involved with adult male offenders. In December 1920 she arrested a 17-year-old boy and a 15-year-old girl—the boy for rape and the girl for slashing his face when she caught him with another girl. Early the following year Grace arrested a 21-year-old man for contributing to the delinquency of a minor.

Grace helped to solve an especially troubling case concerning a 15-year-old girl named Emma who was passing through Chicago in April 1921 with a 45-year-old man. The man said he was Emma's father. Upon closer investigation authorities learned that he had engaged in sexual relations with Emma. He was charged with incest and held for $3,000 bond. Later Emma confided in Grace that the man was *not* her father. He and his wife had kidnapped her from her family's farm home in Arkansas. The man abandoned his wife in Kansas City and forced Emma to continue traveling with him across the country. He had forced Emma to call him Dad and his wife Mom. But Emma wanted desperately to return to her real family. With Grace's intervention, that was possible.

A notorious gang of thieves terrorized the South Side of Chicago for several weeks early in 1922. Storekeepers and residents

JULIA WADES-IN-THE-WATER

She dressed for work in a buckskin dress with a divided skirt, making it easier to ride her horse over the rough terrain of Glacier National Park in Montana in the 1920s and '30s. Her gun was nestled in a holster slung over her shoulder. Julia Wades-in-the-Water was believed to be the only woman serving as an Indian police officer in the world. A member of the Blackfoot nation, she served with pride.

While many of her duties were similar to those of her fellow officers in the nation's cities, she had unique experiences. Her beat covered a huge expanse of rugged, open country. Her form of transportation was a horse. A news reporter described her as "a striking figure" as she patrolled the harsh landscape from atop her horse.

Although she prided herself in using her gun infrequently, she had a reputation as a "crack shot." She could be seen regularly practicing on the target range with her fellow officers. However, Julia said she preferred to use persuasion when handling potential offenders.

Julia retired from her service in the 1930s after 25 years as a policewoman.

Julia Wades-in-the-Water.
Museum of the Rockies/
William S. Yale

were targets of the gang of four men and two women known as the Black Knights. Finally a break occurred in the case when police captured the women and three of the men. The arrests followed a week that had been rampant with crime. And the police chief as well as local papers praised three policewomen—including Grace—for their participation in the capture of the Black Knights. After the arrests, gang members admitted to committing as many as 20 robberies and burglaries. One of the Black Knights had escaped capture and was still on the run. He was a desperately wanted man, but he eluded capture for months—until late in the fall when he ran into Grace Wilson.

Ira J. Newson had been considered a snappy dresser when he made his living as a Black Knight. No one recognized him with his dirty face and hands and in the overalls he wore as a hand on the Illinois Central Railroad tracks at 26th Street. Every day for months he walked to and from his job, passing the police station on Cottage Grove Avenue. No one knew he was the sole survivor of the gang that had intimidated the South Side of the city for weeks earlier in the year. That is, *almost* no one.

Something about the man who passed the station every day caught Grace's attention. She knew without a doubt that this railroad worker was one of the most wanted men in the city. She went to the police captain and told him about her suspicions. He assigned several policemen to accompany Grace to the house on South Park Street where Newson lived. They surrounded the house, but the Black Knight jumped from a second-story window. A gun battle between Newson and the police ensued. Eventually he was captured and confessed to the crimes. He presumably joined the rest of the Black Knights at their new home in the penitentiary at Joliet, Illinois.

Although Grace had built a reputation for herself as a police-woman who could handle anything that came her way, many of her day-to-day duties involved interactions with far less notorious characters. The *Chicago Defender* newspaper described her as an "invaluable aid to young girls" in giving them advice and "saving many from the primrose path." She interacted with needy families and tried to find help for them with social agencies within the community.

In the spring of 1933 Grace helped a 15-year-old boy who was far from his home in Kentucky. Cecil Barbour was a boy who liked to wander occasionally. He was normally a dependable lad who helped support his widowed mother by selling newspapers back home in Maysville. But Chicago police picked him up at the World's Fair grounds and turned him over to the care of Grace. He admitted he had enjoyed his day at the fair—the culmination of a couple of years on the road. He told Grace that

Grace Wilson (first from left) in a shooting contest for policewomen.
Chicago History Museum, DN-0075400; Chicago Daily News

he had been to New England and the mid-Atlantic states before making his way westward to Chicago but that he had "seen the sights" and was ready to return to his mother.

Grace had developed her shooting skills shortly after her hire in 1918, when her commanding officer told her she needed to learn how to shoot a gun. Two of her fellow officers—John Scott and William Middleton of the detective bureau—spent time teaching her all they knew about handling guns. Before long, she was as skilled as they. In fact, when asked about his fellow policewoman's shooting skills, Officer Middleton joked, "Scott and I are taking lessons from *her* now."

Grace's reputation as a sharpshooter was well established by the time she entered a shooting contest for policewomen sponsored by a local Chicago newspaper in 1924. For the third consecutive year, she took second place in the event, competing with 39 other women. Because of her expertise, she became known as the Annie Oakley of the Chicago Police Department—after the famed Wild West sharpshooter who was popular at the time.

Grace's accomplishments rounding up spitters during the influenza epidemic, capturing murder suspects, saving young kidnap victims, and breaking up gangs earned her an admirable reputation in police circles. African Americans celebrated the appointment of Grace as one of the first black policewomen in the country in 1918. Chicago's black community rejoiced to see their race represented in a city department. But most important of all, young women like Anna, who entered the justice system in 1915 and endured the abuses of the policemen at the Harrison Street Jail, felt just a little less intimidated when they were helped by sympathetic policewomen like Grace Wilson.

LEARN MORE

Chicago History Museum
www.chicagohistory.org

"The Great Migration (1900–1970)," *The Rise and Fall of Jim Crow,* Public Broadcasting Service
www.pbs.org/wnet/jimcrow/stories_events_migration.html

MARY SULLIVAN

· · · · · · · · · · · · · · · ·

No Career for a Lady

"*CARTER'S PILLS PRESENTS* [*POLICE WHISTLE*] Police-woman. [*SINISTER ORGAN MUSIC*] *Based on episodes in the career of Lieutenant Mary Sullivan, for 35 years on the New York City police force. Tonight's program* [*MORE SINISTER ORGAN MUSIC*]: *'The Case of the Scheming Bridegroom'* [*ORGAN MUSIC*]."

This opening of a popular radio program in June 1947 invited listeners to stay tuned for the 15-minute segment depicting a fictional scenario—based on a real crime that New York City police lieutenant Mary Sullivan had solved.

Radio actors read a script that related the story of Bianca Riatzo, a young immigrant woman who had answered an advertisement in a lonely hearts magazine. She had not met the man of her dreams, but her friend Freida thought *she* had when she replied to an ad from a man who wanted a wife. Freida quit her job as a cook at a New York hotel and moved to California to marry the man.

Bianca had not heard from Freida for six months. She feared the worst, and Mary Sullivan confirmed her fears with a phone call to authorities in California. Freida had been murdered, but her murderer had not been apprehended. All police had for evidence was Freida's purse with a man's fingerprints.

And most frightening of all, Bianca had recently answered an ad from the same magazine, and the man who was advertising for a wife appeared to be the man who had enticed Freida to move to California! He was back in New York and looking for another victim.

The radio program paused as the announcer encouraged listeners to "stop dousing their stomachs with soda" and try Carter's Pills to alleviate their "blocked digestive tracks"—a typical commercial break in radio broadcasting.

As the commercial came to a close, *Policewoman* picked up with the actress playing Mary Sullivan answering the magazine ad placed by the suspect. She made plans to go undercover and meet the mysterious man that evening in a restaurant.

By 1947, when *Policewoman* was a popular Sunday evening radio program, Mary Sullivan had retired from the New York City Police Department, was working as a consultant to a detective agency, and played herself at the close of each *Policewoman* broadcast—providing the real-life conclusion to the cases for listeners who anxiously awaited the ending to each mystery.

Mary's 35-year career had begun in 1911 when she arrived at the West 47th Street station in the heart of New York City's Tenderloin section dressed in "a long green gown, picture hat trimmed with white flowers, and a fluffy green parasol." She was a 21-year-old widow with a daughter to support. After several years as a sales clerk in the corset department of a large department store, a stint as a store detective, and a period as a traveling saleswoman, Mary was ready to leave the road to spend more time with her daughter. During her time as a store detective, Mary had met a policewoman who encouraged her to take a civil service exam to join the ranks of the police force. To her surprise, she passed the exam with flying colors and was to report to work.

When she resigned from her position with the department store, her boss remarked, "That's no career for a lady. You'll be disillusioned within a month. I'll keep the position here open for you until you come back." It's uncertain how long he kept the position open, but Mary never returned. Instead, she spent the next 35 years enjoying her career as a policewoman.

The Tenderloin was a notorious section of the city touching on another neighborhood called Hell's Kitchen—which lived up to its name. Both were disreputable hellholes of humanity—filled with dance halls, saloons, dubious rooming houses, and houses of prostitution. A steady stream of drug addicts, prostitutes, shoplifters, drunkards, and chorus girls coursed through the police station where Mary spent her three-month probation. Any female prisoners were put into her care.

One of Mary's first cases involved a woman who was arrested and brought into the station for her participation in a "badger game." Mary assumed this had something to do with the woman "annoying animals at the zoo." However, the unusual term was police slang for a trick used by unscrupulous couples to extort money. An attractive woman lured a man into a hotel room, and when the situation became "compromising," the woman's "husband" or "boyfriend" burst into the room demanding money from the victim. Oftentimes the men were prominent citizens or politicians who did not want their names publicized. Or they were intimidated by physical threats and were happy to pay the sum demanded by the culprits.

Processing female alcoholics who were arrested for disorderly conduct was one of Mary's responsibilities at the Tenderloin station. There never seemed to be a dearth of prisoners entering the station ready to fight the policewoman who dared to remove the half-empty bottle of whiskey from their clutches. Many were perpetual drinkers who Mary saw repeatedly during her time at the Tenderloin station. She harbored little sympathy for some of the offenders, but others tore at her heartstrings, including the woman who said, "It's only when I'm drunk that I can forget. As soon as I get a bit sober I begin to see his face." The woman was talking about her little boy, whom she had accidentally poisoned to death when she mistakenly gave him a toxic tablet in place of his medicine.

Early during her days as a policewoman at the Tenderloin, Mary began to dream of becoming a police detective. It was a secret she couldn't share with anyone, because policewomen were restricted in what they were allowed to do within the department. It would require a small miracle for a woman to enter the ranks of detectives.

After a three-month probation Mary was moved from the West 47th Street station house to another neighborhood that was a step above the nitty-gritty streets of the Tenderloin and Hell's Kitchen. But there were plenty of crimes to go around all the neighborhoods—just different flavors.

The new assignment allowed Mary to get out of the station house and deal with problems within the community—the type of work a police detective would perform. She was sent to Coney Island for the nearly impossible task of clearing the popular amusement park of itinerant people known then as gypsies, who plied their trades of palm-reading and fortune-telling.

She also went into dance halls where Japanese and Chinese men danced with white women (a sight the intolerant public of the time frowned upon) and where the proprietors sold liquor illegally and often employed runaway girls. As time passed and the managers of the halls recognized Mary as a policewoman, they devised a system to alert customers to her arrival. As she stepped in the door, the band suddenly began to play an old-fashioned waltz—a sign for liquor bottles to be stowed out of sight and the dancing to become "proper enough for a party in a church basement."

In this upscale neighborhood unscrupulous men set up businesses to bilk unsuspecting widows out of their life savings. There was one especially devious fellow who the police were having a difficult time catching at his scheme. The police chief decided to put Mary undercover to catch the scoundrel in the act. It turned out to be a milestone in Mary's career.

Mary found the man at his office "behind a mahogany desk large enough for roller skating." Dressed in her posh sealskin coat, she entered the office as a rich widow "of the clinging vine species." She told the swindler her husband had left her with a sizable fortune and she was looking for a place to invest.

The man could hardly contain his glee as he assured Mary he could help her invest in an Arizona gold mine that an Indian chief had supposedly revealed to his brother—who had saved the chief's life. He told Mary that he was offering her this once-in-a-lifetime opportunity because she was so charming. She handed him $200 of marked bills until she could return the next day with the rest. But just as Mary departed, two police detectives burst into the office and apprehended the astonished financial advisor.

Mary had successfully performed the duties of a police detective, and her bosses were ready to reward her. They gave her a commendation and, more important, promoted her to police detective! Even more, she was about to take part in solving one of the most sensational crimes of the time—one that would bring down one of her fellow officers.

In her new duties as a New York City police detective, Mary went undercover to hang out with the wives and girlfriend of three gangsters named Dago Frank, Lefty Louis, and Gyp the Blood. She was an invisible part of the police department's "Strong Arm Squad," headed by Lieutenant Charles Becker, also known as the Magnificent because of his physical beauty and his extreme popularity with the New York public.

In 1912 it was a common practice for illegal establishments to pay protection money to the city's law enforcement officials—in other words, paying off corrupt cops to ensure protection from apprehension. The police chief was determined to clean up his department, and his new female detective could help him do it.

An infamous gambler named Herman Rosenthal paid someone in the police department money to keep his illegal actions quiet. Rumors began to spread that the "someone" was the Magnificent. (Many wondered how the lieutenant had managed to save up $70,000 on a salary of only about $1,600 per year.)

When police raided Rosenthal's place of business, it became evident that a rift had taken place between the gambler and the police officer to whom he had paid protection money. Rosenthal was livid. He had paid a great deal of protection money, and yet police still raided his business. He decided to squeal on the officer—revealing the name of his protector to a grand jury. However, on the day of his scheduled appearance at the courthouse, Rosenthal was having a beer at a restaurant. As he stepped to the curb outside the diner, a dark-colored car pulled up alongside him. Shots were fired from within the vehicle, and Rosenthal lay dead on the sidewalk.

It didn't take long for the authorities to identify four men as suspects. Dago Frank was caught first at the apartment of his ex-girlfriend—a prostitute named Rosie. She was described as a tall girl, "hard as a steel plate," with "hair bleached the color of dried hay and cheeks painted red as a signal flag."

After Dago Frank was thrown in jail, Rosie began bargaining for his release. Although she and the gangster had parted ways when she moved in with Fat Abie Harris, she still harbored romantic feelings for Dago Frank. She told the district attorney she knew plenty about the other three gangsters involved in the Rosenthal shooting—Whitey Lewis, Lefty Louis, and Gyp the Blood. Mary was brought in to become the constant companion of Rosie, who never caught on that Mary was an undercover policewoman—possibly because Rosie was often under the influence of opium.

In time Rosie introduced Mary to Gyp's and Lefty's wives. She began to spend time with them and learned a great deal. She learned the two men were dandies who wore expensive suits, silk socks, and expensive cologne. They also spent time at a bathhouse, and Gyp got a manicure every day.

When Mary wasn't with the women, she was secretly trailing them. They were seldom out of her sight. Eventually, all three gangsters were caught when the police traced a phone call one of the wives made to her husband.

At the trial, witnesses revealed that the Magnificent had indeed hired a gunman to kill Herman Rosenthal to prevent him from naming his police protector. The Magnificent was arrested for his part in the murder and sentenced to death by electric chair.

After her part in the Rosenthal case, Mary's career continued to advance. She spent five years as a detective in Harlem, where she looked for illicit activities in the "torrid dance halls," "clip joints," and "disorderly houses" of the city's "negro colony" from 1913 to 1918. Often she was up all night gathering evidence in the seedier establishments, only to spend the mornings testifying in court, where "expensive and nimble-witted lawyers" tried to trip her up with their "well-laid traps."

On one occasion she and a male detective brought down the nefarious Lenox Avenue Gang—wanted for a variety of crimes— in a disreputable piano bar that the group frequented. As Mary and the undercover detective sat drinking one night, a hush fell over the crowd upon the entry of five "gorilla-like" characters with hats pulled down over their eyes. Her male counterpart discreetly passed her one of his guns and told her she was on her own as he headed for the main room to confront the gangsters. Mary was left alone to handle four burly men who were heading for the doorway for a quick escape. To her surprise, they obeyed as she aimed her gun and commanded, "Everybody against the wall!"

In 1918 Mary experienced one of the major thrills of her life when she was transferred to the New York City Homicide Squad. Here she worked to solve murders committed by the

Pistol practice was part of training for New York City policewomen.
Library of Congress, LC-USZ62-94193

likes of the Hudson Dusters, the Hell's Kitchen Gang, and the San Juan Hill Mob. At the time, the police were handling an average of one murder per day.

Mary spent two years in the homicide squad and was rewarded for her outstanding service when she was chosen to become a member of the elite honor legion of the police department. No woman had ever joined this prestigious group. It was a great accomplishment. But the occasion was tarnished for Mary, as by 1921 she had left the homicide squad and been reassigned to a lowly post as matron at a remote jail in Long Island—a punishment for actions she had taken in her attempt to gain equal rights for women officers. It was a story that would repeat itself many times over the years in many police departments around the country.

Back in 1918 Mary had taken a brazen step in obtaining equal rights for women officers in the New York City Police Department. She had been on the force for about seven years when she decided it was time to do something about the sex discrimination she saw within the force. She formed a group called the Policewomen's Endowment Association, through which she planned to advocate for equal rights.

Women were hired at the level of police matrons rather than patrolmen—putting them at a disadvantage. They were paid less than male officers. They also had no opportunities for promotion to higher positions, and their retirement pensions were much lower than men's.

As president of the Policewomen's Endowment Association, Mary decided to take her complaints to the New York State Assembly in Albany. She lobbied assemblymen to pass a law that changed the official designation from *police matron* to *policewoman*, giving women officers the same salaries and pensions as patrolmen. It was a victory for policewomen, but her

MARY HOLLAND: FINGERPRINT EXPERT

"Why when a woman does some difficult thing well should it be considered different? There is no work a man does that a woman cannot do just as well," declared Mary Holland. She was talking about her skills as a fingerprint expert.

Mary and her husband owned a private detective agency in Chicago in the early 1900s, and she had studied under two of the world's most renowned fingerprint experts in the world—Frenchman Alphonse Bertillon and Englishman John Ferrier of Scotland Yard. In 1912 a newspaper described her as "among the foremost living authorities on the thumb print system of identification."

In addition to solving crimes at her detective agency, Mary was frequently called by the Chicago police to help solve exceptionally confounding murder cases because of her invaluable skills.

She explained to a reporter that while faces changed with age, fingerprints remained the same and no two persons have fingerprints just alike. "It's an infallible means of identification and the neatest and prettiest of any system that was ever conceived," she said.

Mary explained that while some shrewd criminals think they will fool law enforcers by mutilating their thumbs, it's not a solution to their problems. When the flesh heals, the imprint grows back to its original impression. "It is absolutely impossible to change their appearance," Mary explained.

Shutterstock

audacity had angered her bosses back at the department. Their displeasure with Mary's brashness resulted in her demotion and banishment to Long Island.

Fortunately, Mary's exile ended in 1926 when a newly appointed police commissioner offered her the opportunity to head up the women's bureau—a separate division within the department. It wasn't an entirely new division, as it had existed before—having been formed in 1918 but shut down in 1924. It was to be newly organized—this time under the direction of Mary Sullivan.

Mary's reemergence as a key figure in the New York City Police Department set the stage for the next 20 years. As head of the women's bureau, Mary was promoted to lieutenant and earned a salary of $3,300 per year. She was in charge of 150 policewomen. Their duties involved putting fortune-tellers out

Mary Sullivan.
New York City Police Department Museum

of business; apprehending shoplifters; and helping to convict sex offenders, drug users, and drug dealers.

In 1929 Mary was well established in her position when an incident at a birth control clinic temporarily sidetracked her career. At the time, birth control was a very controversial topic. Although it was not illegal to operate a birth control clinic that catered to *married* women, it was against the law to give birth control devices to *unmarried* women.

In the spring of 1929 Mary received information leading her to believe a clinic on West 15th Street was serving unmarried women. There were different versions of what happened when the police—including the head of the women's bureau—raided the clinic. Police arrested several staff members and carried them off in the patrol wagon. The head of the clinic said the police confiscated private medical files of all the patients—which would have been illegal. Mary denied this and said she took only the file—intended for use in court—of an undercover policewoman who had been "treated" at the clinic.

In the end Mary's supervisor did not stand behind her. He said she had conducted the raid without his knowledge. Some New Yorkers believed Mary conducted the raid because she belonged to the Catholic Church, which disapproved of birth control. Mary was relieved of her duty as head of the women's bureau, but only for a few months. After the excitement died down, she was reinstated and continued to serve as head of the women's bureau until her retirement in 1946. She had proven that police work *was* a career for a lady.

LEARN MORE

"History," by Jeffery G. Barnes, *Fingerprint Sourcebook* (National Criminal Justice Reference Service, International Association for Identification, et al., July 2011)
www.ncjrs.gov/pdffiles1/nij/225321.pdf

Old Time Radio Downloads
www.oldtimeradiodownloads.com

PART III

·················

THE DIFFERENCE A WORD CAN MAKE

Police Officers

IN 1942 THE NEW YORK City Police Department issued a new piece of equipment to its policewomen—a combination gun holster/makeup kit. It would make it easier for "the pistol-packin' mammas" to carry their "shooting iron" along with their powder puffs. The black cowhide bag with an envelope flap swung from the shoulder and was equipped with the regulation Colt .32-caliber revolver, a plastic compact, dry rouge case, lipstick, and a compartment for gloves, money, and a handkerchief. Well intentioned or patronizing? Whatever one's view, in the mid-20th century female police were still treated differently from their male colleagues.

In the late 1960s and early 1970s a series of legal actions—passage of laws and court rulings—changed the face of the modern workplace significantly. Federal legislation trickled down to the state and local levels, changing practices in cities, towns, and rural areas across the country and impacting public and private employers. The Equal Employment Opportunity Act (EEOA), passed in March 1972, prohibited employment discrimination at state and local levels on the basis of race, color, religion, sex, or national origin.

This meant women could not be treated differently merely because of their gender. In the world of law enforcement it meant women could go on patrol, could apply for promotions with fellow male officers, and were entitled to the same salaries as men. Previously, women typically were not allowed duty in patrol cars, could not apply for positions that had been open only to males, and received lower salaries than men while doing the same type of work. Physical requirements—which many argued were not relevant to good police work—kept women from applying for many jobs. For example, height and weight requirements blocked many women from positions within police departments. Sometimes demands for specific experience stopped women from applying for jobs; however, they lacked the experience because department policies prevented them from taking jobs that would give them the necessary experience!

Yet with the passage of the new legislation, the role of female police officers began to evolve. And by the time Julia Grimes and Moira Smith became police officers, their equipment reflected the changes that had occurred in regard to their duties. Both carried weapons and trained in the use of firearms—and neither carried a powder puff or rouge with them on the job!

LITTLE WORD, BIG IMPACT

In 1964 American women learned the power of a little word in an act of the US Congress.

Early in 1964 the House of Representatives was debating the Civil Rights Act of 1964. President John F. Kennedy introduced the bill in 1963 as an attempt to guarantee African Americans basic rights in the workplace and public places such as restaurants, bus stations, and swimming pools. While Congress had not passed it when the president was assassinated in November 1963, after his death the nation was ready to honor the slain president with the passage of civil rights legislation.

In February 1964 US Representative Howard W. Smith from Virginia introduced the word *sex* into the newly proposed act, which would result in prohibiting discrimination based on gender as well as race. The House of Representatives—mostly male—broke into laughter. The debate continued for two hours—most of it in a jocular manner, as few took the idea seriously. Some historians believe Smith added the word *sex* because he was certain it would derail the entire act. Even congressmen who endorsed a civil rights act to support rights for African Americans would oppose an act that included women. But Smith was wrong. The bill—with the tiny word *sex* added—passed both houses of Congress and was signed into law in July 1964.

Women could no longer lose their jobs when they got married, they could no longer be denied jobs because they had young children, and it was now illegal to fire a woman because she became pregnant. Moreover, police departments could no longer advertise "male only" positions.

MOIRA SMITH

....

A Love Story

"IF MY MOM WAS BACK for an hour, I'd talk about everything that's going on in my life and get her advice, because I feel like her opinion could really help me figure things out," Patricia Smith muses as she talks about the mother she never knew.

Although 16-year-old Patricia doesn't remember her mother, Moira Smith, friends and family have provided her with countless stories that have made it easy for her to fall in love with the mother she lost because of the 9/11 attacks in 2001, when Patricia was two. They refer to Patricia's habit of rolling her eyes when her dad, Jim Smith, does something to exasperate her. Moira did the same. And although Patricia did not inherit her mom's blonde hair and blue eyes, she shares Moira's philosophy of life.

"Life can be annoying and unfair at times, but it can also be wonderful and happy. I really try to look at things from different points of view so I can get some understanding of how that all works—I owe that all to her, I guess," Patricia says. "Losing my mom has made me realize that things could be better, but they could also be worse."

Many of the stories about Moira have come to Patricia from Kathleen Conaghan and Cathy Gallogly, two of Moira's closest friends. The Three Musketeers—as most everyone in the neighborhood referred to the three girls—met at the age of five. They lived on the same tree-lined street in Brooklyn, New York, in a neighborhood of first-generation immigrant families—many from Ireland, like Moira's family. The three met in kindergarten, and their friendship grew throughout middle and high school.

The Three Musketeers' relationship was cemented in long, hot summer days playing stickball, Wiffle ball, softball, and tennis. With only one bike among them, two girls balanced precariously on the fender and handlebars while one steered from the seat. They attended Mets baseball games together. Sometimes Moira's mom packed the neighborhood kids into the car for the short drive to Rockaway Beach. Sledding and ice-skating filled the winter months.

When the very scary movie *Jaws* was released in the summer of 1975, Kathleen and Moira happened to be visiting Moira's grandparents in Bloomsburg, Pennsylvania. The girls spent an entire day sitting in the front row with their backs to the screen so they could watch the other moviegoers "freak out." Back home in Brooklyn they played extras in the John Travolta movie *Saturday Night Fever.* And the three spent a good amount of their time playing cops and robbers with the neighborhood boys—the girls being the cops. During these early years as kids Kathleen and Cathy witnessed the first inkling of a love that Moira would carry to the last day of her life—helping people and saving lives through police work.

It was when Kathleen and Moira were at camp in seventh grade that Moira demonstrated her ability to think quickly and instinctively rush to aid someone in need of help. To pass the swimming test, the girls had to swim across the pool. Kathleen wasn't sure she could make it, so she asked Moira to get in line immediately behind her. Kathleen did make it to the far side of the pool, but as she turned to watch her friend begin the test, she saw another girl had "budged" in line between her and Moira. And the girl was having trouble—it became apparent that she was drowning. Before a lifeguard could jump in to help the struggling swimmer, Moira had pulled the girl to safety, saving the girl's life!

When it came time to go to college, Kathleen and Moira enrolled together at Niagara University in Upstate New York, while Cathy stayed in Brooklyn to help care for young siblings after her mother died. By this time Moira had already decided to pursue the only career she had ever considered—police work. She chose a major in criminal justice. She put her dreams on hold for a time to help care for her mother, who became gravely ill. But after her mother's death, Moira entered the New York Police Department Academy.

At the academy, Moira completed the training to become an officer for the New York City Police Department. She took self-defense, firearms training, boxing, and driver training. She studied criminal law procedures, police and social sciences, and New York State penal law. She learned about rules and regulations and how to complete the day-to-day paperwork of the department. She made many friends, and in December 1988 Moira left the academy ready to begin the career she had always wanted.

"She took my Yankee hat off and tossed it across the room. She was a Mets fan," Jim Smith said about the first time he met his future wife. Both were New York City police officers, and they soon became a couple. Jim fell in love with Moira's adventurous spirit and her passion for travel. They took much-needed breaks from police work with vacations in England, Ireland, France, Belgium, and Monte Carlo. Moira rode a camel in Tangiers, and together they ran with the bulls in Pamplona, Spain.

"As we waited with thousands of other people for the bulls, we could see the people in front of us begin to turn and run at us in a mixture of joy and sheer terror," Jim recalled. "Why did she do it? For the simple thrill of it. She also enjoyed the pageantry and spectacle of it all."

The exciting holidays were interludes to the day-to-day work of policing the most populated city in the United States. Moira's first assignment was policing the subways that snaked under the city. It was a dangerous job, but her fellow officers said she was a good cop "who was always on top of things."

"A crush of sheared metal and battered passengers."

"The first car was sheared in half lengthwise . . . striking the wall of the subway tunnel . . . slashing through steel beams."

"A tangled metal mass."

These and other reports in August 1991 described "the worst New York subway disaster in 63 years," which occurred just as Moira was heading home after an eight-and-a-half-hour tour. As she ran through the Union Square station, she encountered a motorman, who Moira learned later had been driving the train. She asked what had happened, and when she learned details of the crash, she ran into the tunnel to assist in rescuing passengers trapped underground. Throughout the early morning hours Moira helped set up a triage unit and administered first aid to victims. After working for 24 hours straight, Moira finally went to the hospital to be treated for smoke inhalation.

Charges were brought against the motorman when police determined that he had been drinking and left the scene of the accident. Moira's testimony helped convict the man. He was sentenced to 15 years in prison. She received the police department's Distinguished Duty Medal for saving dozens of lives that day.

For a time Moira worked in the 13th Precinct Street Narcotics Enforcement Unit (SNEU)—a plainclothes unit that dealt with low-level narcotic trafficking. It was her job to arrest people she witnessed buying and selling drugs. One day a fellow officer brought Moira a business card that was intended for buyers of marijuana. The card promised, "We deliver." When Moira called the phone number on the card and asked to buy the drug, the man on the phone indeed agreed to deliver at a designated location. He described the vehicle he would be driving, and Moira made arrangements to meet the drug dealer. She called for assistance from a fellow officer who was patrolling in the area—her husband, Jim!

When the vehicle approached the location where Moira waited, Jim was ready to stop the driver on reasonable suspicion. And as Moira opened the door of the suspicious vehicle, an overwhelming aroma of marijuana greeted her. This gave the officers probable cause to search the vehicle, and they proceeded to do so but found no drugs.

Moira and the other officers were perplexed. Then she turned on the air-conditioning controls—but no air came out. That's when she pulled off the vents and began to pull out bag after bag of marijuana from the dashboard!

By 1999 Moira and Jim had a daughter, Patricia, and Moira was ready for a change in her policing duties. She moved into community policing, where she had fewer chances of interacting with dangerous criminals. She worked to control crowds at labor disputes and protest rallies. She visited shut-ins who needed attention or who just wanted to talk, and she took elderly

New York City street scene on September 11, 2001.
Courtesy of the Prints and Photographs Division, Library of Congress

citizens on shopping trips in the police van. She also represented the police department at community meetings.

Moira was patrolling the 13th precinct on September 11, 2001, when she witnessed a plane striking one of the two World Trade Center towers. After sending a radio message to headquarters (the first officer to do so), she gathered other witnesses and took them to the precinct station before rushing downtown to the towers. Many of the details of that day and Moira's experiences will never be known, but survivors and a picture have told part of her story. One man told of seeing Moira directing throngs of people as they made their way down the stairways of the South Tower. She kept the crowds moving, using her flashlight and baton to wave people along. He said Moira seemed "in control of the situation" as she repeated over and over, "Don't look! Keep moving."

Moira Smith and Edward Nicholls.
Corey Sipkin, New York Daily News, *Getty Images*

Edward Nicholls was making his way from his office on the 102nd floor of the South Tower when Moira spotted him. He had been injured and was with a group of people when she took his arm and guided him out of the building to a triage area. A photographer captured a picture of the two—the last photo taken of Moira, who was killed by the soon-to-collapse building. She was the only female NYPD officer killed on 9/11.

Edward's time with Moira was brief and chaotic. He struggles to find words to describe the encounter: "No words are appropriate. She showed tremendous courage—and made the ultimate sacrifice. A heart of gold." In those few moments, a stranger had captured the essence of Moira.

Moira's childhood friend Kathleen Conaghan had known Moira most of her life. "Until every person was out, I knew she would be there," she says about her friend's actions at the World Trade Center.

As the tragedy unfolded that day, Kathleen thought about Moira saving the girl who almost drowned at summer camp and her determination to follow her dream of becoming a police officer so she could help others. She thought about their last visit, when she "gave Moira a big hug and said, 'I love you.'"

Moira Smith followed her dream to a career she loved. And although it ended in a tragedy, she is kept alive through the strangers whose lives she touched and through the friends and family who gave Patricia the mother she never knew.

What if by some miracle Kathleen was given one more precious hour with her friend? She says, "I would take one minute and give the rest to her daughter, Patricia."

ARTIFACTS TELL A STORY

The National September 11 Memorial Museum opened in May 2014. The goal of museum designers was to "create a meaningful tribute to the victims without traumatizing the visitors." With so many victims (over 3,000 individuals died that day) and innumerable images from the tragedy, it became a tremendous challenge. In the end the designers chose large and small artifacts to help visitors to the museum appreciate the valor and the trauma of the days and weeks that followed the terrorist attack.

The museum houses two fire trucks and an ambulance along with a 60-ton, 40-foot-tall steel column salvaged from the structure. It is covered in spray-painted messages to the dead, messages left by the men and women who aided in the cleanup at the site. The museum also holds the Slurry Wall, a 3-foot-thick concrete barrier that held up the foundations of the two towers. A 15-inch-high sentence fashioned out of steel recovered from the Twin Towers reminds visitors that "no day shall erase you from the memory of time."

Among the many smaller artifacts at the museum are personal items donated by victims' families. And amid the thousands of items in the exhibition, visitors will find a small lapel police badge with the number 13—identifying the precinct of its owner—and a battered police badge with the number 10467—Moira Smith's number.

LEARN MORE

National September 11 Memorial and Museum
www.911memorial.org

National Commission on Terrorist Attacks
upon the United States
www.9-11commission.gov

JULIA GRIMES

Changing Course

"MY DAD AGREED TO LET me take a five-dollar introductory ride in a Cessna 150, assuming I would get airsick and that would be the end of it," Julia Canter Grimes laughs. But 14-year-old Julia was just beginning her lifelong love of flying in the 1970s.

"I spent every dime of my allowance and my earnings from all my after-school jobs to pay for a lesson once or twice a month," she adds. By the time she was 16 she took her first solo flight, and on her 17th birthday she obtained her private license. Her high school yearbook picture shows Julia holding an old wooden propeller. "All I wanted to do was fly for a living," she says.

As a student at Sewickley Academy near Pittsburgh, Pennsylvania, Julia was given a book from a teacher as a thank-you for serving as stage manager for a school production. *The Last of the Bush Pilots* was set in Alaska, and the book shaped Julia's career aspirations. "I read it and became infatuated with the mystique, freedom, and challenge of bush flying," she says.

"It seemed very far away at the time, but little did I know that Alaska would someday be my home and the source of a lifetime of adventures and memories."

As Julia's high school days drew to a close, she began to look for aviation programs at several colleges. She started in Florida but eventually graduated from Parks College of Aeronautical Technology in St. Louis, Missouri. At age 19 she had earned a flight instructor certificate and started teaching flying back in the Pittsburgh area. Gaining experience in the air was key to a career in aviation, so Julia got her multiengine rating and took a job flying copilot in a small twin-engine plane hauling cargo at night—for no pay!

At the same time, Julia started sending applications to all the major airlines. She knew she didn't have enough experience, but says, "My strategy was to be the persistent pilot who applied over and over in the hopes they would eventually hire me."

In 1978 United Airlines hired Julia and assigned her as a Boeing 727 flight engineer (or second officer). She lived on Long Island, New York, and flew out of LaGuardia, Kennedy, and Newark airports. She was thrilled for the opportunity, but world events interfered. It was the early 1980s, and war in the Middle East contributed to fuel shortages and extremely high fuel prices. These factors led to financial woes for the airline industries, and by 1981 Julia found herself furloughed and looking for work.

She decided it was an opportune time to obtain another rating—one that allowed her to fly floatplanes. This led to a job as an air taxi/charter pilot serving the Long Island area and the entire Northeast. Her regular customers included five stockbrokers who commuted to and from Manhattan every day. She flew them into the East River, often under the Brooklyn and Manhattan Bridges, and dropped them off at a dock located at

Wall Street. After the 12-mile, 12-minute flight—a two-hour commute by car—the brokers walked to their offices. Then Julia picked them up at the end of the day.

Julia loved her air taxi job, but it was only seasonal—summer and early fall—so she took a job with the Federal Aviation Administration doing clerical work during the off-season. It was here that Julia met someone who put her in touch with an individual who had a flight school and charter business in Fairbanks, Alaska. Thinking about the book *The Last of the Bush Pilots*, Julia made a call to Fairbanks; and by the end of the phone call, she had been hired to teach flying lessons in Alaska!

For the first six months of 1982 Julia fulfilled her commitment to teach in Fairbanks—many times in −30 degree weather. But it wasn't the cold that caused Julia to change course. "Surrounded by too much land—although beautiful land—I wanted seaplanes again," she says. So in the spring she made her way south to Ketchikan, along the Tongass Narrows, where she was offered a job flying seaplanes again.

Julia found herself going to places with intriguing names like Klawock, Hydaburg, and Metlakatla. She marveled at the exhilarating scenery and was captivated by the people she carried into some of the most remote and beautiful places in America. It was not unusual for Alaska fish and wildlife troopers to use the air taxi service to travel deep into the bush. On those trips the troopers tried to recruit Julia, saying, "We need pilots, and we need women." Julia fit the description.

Julia's chance encounter with the troopers high above the Alaskan wilderness propelled her to a "most unexpected change of course," a change that became what Julia described as "the most remarkable experience" of her life.

Before anyone could become an Alaska state trooper, he or she had to complete intensive training. Recruits spent 14 weeks

Julia Grimes, Alaska state trooper pilot.
Courtesy of Julia Grimes

learning how to do all the things that would be expected of them as troopers. Training took place in Sitka, Alaska—situated on an island in the midst of a spruce and hemlock rainforest. The future troopers shared the island with deer, bears, and other wildlife.

Julia began her training in January 1983. She recalled starting at 5 AM, "doing pushups and running in formation" with her fellow recruits through the trails of Totem Park in the dark and rain and snow. By 10 AM they were in the gym for an hour of "aerobic death—old-fashioned calisthenics." In addition to the physical testing, they underwent schooling in law, criminal investigation, and police procedures. Learning to shoot guns was also part of the training. Shooting was completely new to Julia, and the firearms training became a "stressful challenge."

Having survived the training academy and making the grade, Julia was officially commissioned as an Alaska state trooper. Her first assignment was patrol duty on the swing shift—late into the night, responding to various calls for service and arresting intoxicated drivers. During this first year as a trooper, the colonel (the head of the agency) asked her to participate in a top-secret drug investigation—with suspects who included lobbyists and state legislators!

Julia's participation in Operation Snow White began in November 1983 when she went undercover as a bar waitress in a known drug hangout in Juneau. It meant she had to cut ties with friends and not tell anyone about her assignment. She even had to "resign" from her position with the Alaska State Troopers (AST) to make her new "job" appear authentic. It was so top secret that her immediate supervisor didn't know about her undercover assignment. When she told him she was quitting the AST after only a few months as a trooper, he told her that he considered her to be ungrateful for the investment of time and energy to train her to be a trooper.

The AST had received information that certain legislators might be using cocaine and that lobbyists were thought to be providing them drugs to potentially influence legislation. Julia would work with an outside undercover investigator—called N361—hired by the AST. It was Julia and N361's job to identify people on the street who were selling drugs and make small buys in order to establish their credibility.

After a little more than a year, things were going well, as the drug dealers had accepted Julia and her "boyfriend"—N361—into their circle. But the complete undercover operation almost came to a bad end on New Year's Eve 1984 when someone who had known Julia when she was a pilot in Ketchikan announced to everyone in the bar that she was a trooper!

"Some very good acting and tears managed to convince my boss that, yes, I had been hired by the troopers but was fired for smoking marijuana and was now just trying to make a living and pay bills," Julia explains. "She bought it, and eventually I was back in good graces, and folks started selling me drugs."

Ultimately Julia and N361 orchestrated a house party for their drug-dealing "friends." While alcohol consumers were partying downstairs, cocaine users were steered to an upstairs bedroom equipped with hidden cameras and audio equipment. This resulted in the collection of video evidence and physical evidence of cocaine use by several individuals connected to lobbyists and politicians in Juneau.

Julia and N361 used "tooters," or drinking straws filled with a combination of cotton and petroleum jelly, to collect a sample of white powder without it ever getting into their noses as they "snorted" in view of the drug dealers. They would snort, head to the bathroom, where they put the tooters into evidence bags, and slip them under the door of a locked bedroom where other troopers were collecting and documenting the evidence.

Through Operation Snow White, 21 people were indicted and ultimately convicted of possession and/or distribution of cocaine and marijuana. Although they were never able to connect the drug deals to any legislators, several prominent lobbyists—with close connections to legislators—were convicted. (The trooper who oversaw the investigation was Sgt. Jim Grimes, who later became Julia's husband.)

For Julia this was the beginning of a long-term stint in the Alaska Statewide Drug Enforcement Unit as an investigator. For 12 years she did mobile and aerial surveillance and undercover work to bust drug dealers and traffickers. During this time she shared the workload with some amazing partners, one of whom was a scent detection K-9 named Yambo.

When she was undercover, Julia drew upon skills she didn't know she had. "Undercover work is so different from patrol, as it is fluid, dynamic, and proactive by nature. I learned that because of the less structured environment, I had to be more focused and concentrate on every move I made," she says. "I

YAMBO, THE FINEST OF DOGS

"He is credited with the detection and seizure of illegal drugs with a street value of several million dollars," Julia says about her German shepherd drug detection canine named Yambo. "We seized a lot of dope, he and I."

Yambo was a busy dog during his drug detection days. He could sniff out marijuana, cocaine, heroin, and methamphetamines. He and Julia worked with FedEx, UPS, and US Postal Service inspectors to detect drugs in small packages, and at airports he sniffed for drugs on people and in their luggage.

One time Yambo was called to look for drugs on an oceangoing freighter headed out to sea. He traveled by helicopter from Dutch Harbor, Alaska, to the location of the freighter far out in the ocean and had to be lowered to a small boat. From there he was hauled up the side of the huge ship. "It didn't even faze him," Julia says. "He just started searching for dope when he hit the deck."

Yambo was a hit with kids when he traveled with Julia to remote villages on school visits. They threw his tennis ball, and he'd chase it and bring it back to the kids every time, dropping it at their feet. "If they didn't pick it up soon enough, he would use his right foot to push it to them—every time," Julia laughs.

When Julia transported prisoners in her plane, she always told them Yambo would bite them if they misbehaved. "Truth be told, he wasn't protection trained, but they never knew that," Julia says. She adds, "He was the finest of dogs."

learned quickly that you really have to be an actress while undercover."

Those skills served her well during a cocaine investigation she was working with a partner. The two were meeting with a coke dealer at his house in Anchorage. While Julia was using the bathroom, she placed her gun—a Smith & Wesson Detective Special she had concealed in the back of her jeans—between towels that were folded and stacked on the back of the toilet. She went back into the living room, where her partner and the coke dealer were scheduling a future meeting to purchase the drugs. The dealer mentioned a favorite book, *Snowblind: A Brief Career in the Cocaine Trade* by Robert Sabbag. He offered to lend it to Julia as a how-to guide, and she was eager to take it because it could be used as evidence.

After Julia and her partner had left the house and were a short distance down the road, she realized she had forgotten to take her gun from the towels in the bathroom. "Many emotions occurred simultaneously—panic, embarrassment, and fear," Julia says.

Luckily, the dealer had forgotten to give Julia his "guidebook to drug dealing," so she had a believable excuse for going back to the house. The two undercover troopers headed back to retrieve the book, and while she was there, Julia asked to use the bathroom, where she found her gun still safely concealed in the towels.

Julia recalls another incident that wasn't quite as successful for the troopers. While she was in the Statewide Drug Enforcement Unit in the mid-1980s, she and a partner were assigned to look for indoor and outdoor marijuana "grow operations" near Fairbanks using the AST helicopter. They spotted a field of what they thought was marijuana. Several signs made them suspicious—the color of the plants and the distance of the field from the residence, among other things.

DARE: ALASKA STYLE

Drug Abuse Resistance Education (DARE) is designed to give schoolkids in kindergarten through 12th grade skills they need to avoid drugs, gangs, and violence. Today it also involves Internet safety and bullying awareness. The program is delivered to school districts by law enforcement officials across the United States and in other countries across the globe. It was started in 1983 in Los Angeles.

It wouldn't be unusual to see a police squad car parked in any school parking lot as DARE officers deliver their messages helping kids resist peer pressure and live drug-free and violence-free lives.

Julia Grimes taught the DARE program at the tiny village of Aleknagik, Alaska, located on the Wood

Julia and Yambo leave for a DARE presentation.
Courtesy of Julia Grimes

River in the far southwestern part of the state. The school building was on the north shore of the river, but many of the kids lived on the south shore. And when Julia came to deliver the DARE program, she drove to the south shore in her truck. Then she and the school kids living on the south shore boarded the school bus to travel across the river to the school building.

Their "bus" varied with the seasons. In the warmer months Julia and the kids (and Yambo, Julia's canine partner) squeezed into an open aluminum skiff to head across to the northern shore. In winter they all piled into an oversized dogsled pulled across the frozen river by a snow machine.

"It was probably the most unique delivery of DARE anywhere!" Julia remarks.

The AST obtained a search warrant from a judge and made plans to raid the enterprise. A member of the media was invited to ride along and report on the newsworthy event. As Julia and the other officers began to descend in the helicopter, the civilian pilot exclaimed, "Those are potato plants!"

"And sure enough, we had just raided a potato field in Fairbanks, Alaska, with the media on board!" Julia laughs.

Julia's love of flying in extreme situations made her especially valuable to her law enforcement colleagues. In addition to her enthusiasm, she had plenty of air time. She had racked up 2,800 hours of flying experience with air taxis, using aircraft equipped with both wheels and floats—extremely useful in Alaska's treacherous landscape. In 1984 Julia became the first female trooper/pilot for AST.

One of her assignments over the years was law enforcement in the rural areas, or "bush," of Alaska. She policed isolated, remote villages and communities—the majority of which were only accessible by air or snowmobile. The work required a skilled flier to navigate the often perilous weather situations to respond to criminal activity in the villages or to perform search and rescue in the vast wilderness of her patrol area.

Julia's patrol vehicle in the bush was a Cessna 185 equipped with large wheels in summer for unimproved landing areas, such as beaches and gravel areas, and wheel-skis in the winter for equally unimproved, frozen, snow-covered landing areas. She flew it daily to the outlying native villages to conduct trooper business—investigations, arrests, and school visits. "I picked up many a dead body in that airplane and transported them to the morgue at the Dillingham hospital," Julia recalls.

She remembers responding to a call of an injured snowmobiler who had crashed his machine in a very remote area and needed to be medevaced to the hospital. Julia flew in to the area, communicating with the victim's friends by VHF radio. She landed her Cessna 185 (equipped with skis) uphill on the side of a mountain slope. After loading the victim, the friends helped Julia turn the plane around by hand, and she took off downslope. The victim recovered from his injuries in the hospital.

Oftentimes the rescue missions had happy endings. But Julia recalled one harrowing rescue that had an upsetting conclusion. One day as she made her way back to her home base in her plane, she got a call that a small aircraft had crashed near a tiny village in the tundra. As she turned her plane around and made her way to the site, she realized she didn't have much daylight left.

When she reached the site, landed on a nearby frozen pond, and saw the flames, she knew it was unlikely there could be survivors. Using her fire extinguisher, she managed to put out the flames. As soon as the heat had subsided, she made her way to the smoldering pile and removed the remains of the pilot and passenger. Before she could place them in her plane, she had to let them cool on the barren tundra. Although daylight was disappearing and she didn't want to take off in the dark, she knew how important it would be for the families of the crash victims to have their loved ones. It was an experience that always stayed with Julia. It underscored the fact that life in the bush could be brutal and unforgiving.

After seven years in the bush, Julia was sent to work in Anchorage. In her new position she handled major crimes and dealt with murderers, rapists, and child abusers.

In 2003, after 20 years as an Alaska state trooper, Julia was promoted to the rank of captain. She was the first female trooper to reach the position. Soon after, she was to attain another major milestone in her life and in Alaska's state history.

Julia's time as a captain was very short. After only a few months she was asked to compete for the AST director position and was ultimately appointed by the governor. Her rank would be colonel. Never before had a woman reached the rank of colonel, and never had the agency been headed by a woman.

As the director of the state troopers, Julia was able to rely on all her experiences as a trooper herself. She oversaw the work of 400 law enforcement personnel. She directed the work the agency would tackle. And she wasn't shy about taking on big tasks.

Under Julia's lead the agency reopened cold cases that had been dormant for years. The cold case homicide unit worked to uncover new evidence in these long-forgotten cases and together with the state district attorney brought about arrests in cases thought to be unsolvable. Julia said the unit was eager to unearth evidence that would help to prosecute suspects "who think they have gotten away with murder." She also praised the expertise and commitment of the cold case investigators, as it was meticulous work.

As director, Julia oversaw the investigation of an international drug trafficking ring. Alaska State Troopers worked together with federal investigators and the Royal Canadian Mounted Police. The ring had imported $10 million worth of drugs from British Columbia over a five-year period. They concealed the drugs in secret compartments in vehicles that they drove over the border from Canada. The troopers confiscated the drugs, along with other loot—cash, gold bullion, machine guns, race cars, and real estate. It was a huge bust for the troopers, and Julia applauded the work her team had done. She also had a word of caution for other criminals.

"I'm very proud of my troopers," she said. But she knew their work was not done. She promised that her troopers would find drug traffickers "wherever they are in the state. . . . We intend to find them."

In 1982 when Julia gave those troopers a ride in her air taxi and they enticed her to choose a career as an Alaska state trooper, she knew she was heading into territory that was uncharted for her. She didn't know that she would also make history for women in the state of Alaska.

When she reflected on her career, Julia described it as "an adventure" that gave her the "opportunity to do things the average person doesn't get to do."

Julia's dad was wrong about his daughter when he predicted that at the age of 14 she would take one flying lesson, get airsick, and forget all about flying. Despite his earlier misjudgment, he was on target when he told her, "You can do anything you want to do."

LEARN MORE

The Last of the Bush Pilots by Harmon Helmericks (Random House, 1969)

Wheels Up by Sandi Sumner (Bookstand, 2011)

Women Aviators: 26 Stories of Pioneer Flights, Daring Missions, and Record-Setting Journeys by Karen Bush Gibson (Chicago Review Press, 2013)

PART IV

....

ALL HAIL

========================

Police Chiefs

SHE FIRED THE "OLD BACHELORS" from the force and generally "turned the town upside down." *And* she made the police
force "doff hats to her." Quite a list of accomplishments for a
woman whom newspapers called the "first woman to hold the
position of police commissioner" in Leavenworth, Kansas, in
1894. All of this while, "against the gibes and witticisms of the
public press," showing a "capacity and aptitude for the position"
that "practically silenced all opposition."

Her name was Eva M. Blackman, and she was only 27 years
old. She started out as a stenographer but eventually bought a
labor newspaper called the *Labor News* and published it single-
handedly. She was described as "small of stature," and—as was
often the case when discussing professional women—reporters
felt her attire was also a point of interest. One notified readers
that the new commissioner "believes that comfort should be
paramount to style."

Most people wouldn't recognize her name, and she has long been forgotten by police historians. However, it is because of the perseverance and determination of women like Eva that women today can become chiefs of law enforcement agencies. Eva was fighting the press and her subordinate officers in the 19th century. In the 20th century women like Rhoda Milliken and Penny Harrington were facing the same issues. Today in the 21st century women face some of the same challenges to become leaders in law enforcement.

It wasn't completely unheard of to have women heading up departments—Rhoda Milliken was head of a woman's bureau in Washington, DC, in 1932. But there was a clear distinction: all of her subordinates were women—she supervised no men. Penny Harrington, on the other hand, headed up an entire force, including men.

Today—as in the past—men dominate law enforcement. Only about 13 percent of all police officers are women. Just 7.3 percent of the top command posts (captains and above) are held by women. However, it's not all doom and gloom. Changes have occurred. The media, including television and movies, have evolved in their portrayals of women in law enforcement—showing them as competent, valuable professionals rather than exceptions to the norm. This has helped to promote more favorable attitudes in the general public. The idea of women officers being able to handle violent situations is more accepted. In addition, female officers have more supports in place, including local, regional, and national associations that offer education, information, and guidance to rookie and veteran officers. And many more police departments recognize the benefit of hiring women and have turned to actively recruiting women officers.

RHODA MILLIKEN

....

A Woman with a Beautiful Soul

RHODA MILLIKEN WAS "dolled up like a Christmas tree," wearing "enough rouge to flag a train" when she stepped up to the door of an apartment in the northwest part of Washington, DC, at 1 AM on March 2, 1919.

"Riley," Rhoda Milliken said as she knocked on the door. It was a secret password that was guaranteed to give her entry into the party. It worked. The door swung open, and Rhoda, along with five of her "friends," burst into the apartment.

However, the newly arrived group of two men and four women didn't come to party but rather entered with revolvers drawn, quickly rounding up partygoers before they could flee into the night. It was Prohibition, a time when the sale and manufacture of alcohol was prohibited. The group arrested two revelers for selling liquor and took others into custody as witnesses.

The successful raid conducted under the leadership of policewoman Rhoda Milliken was the culmination of a night of dancing and partying by the policewomen—posing as undercover

Rhoda Milliken.
Reprinted with permission of the DC Public Library, Star Collection, © Washington Post

partygoers. All four were fox-trotting like crazy when one overheard her dance partner tell someone, "Kid, if you go to an apartment in the Woodford apartment house and say 'Riley,' you'll get all the booze you want."

The information was furtively passed among the four policewomen, and they made plans to go to the Woodford apartments. Along the way the women picked up two male officers to make the arrests. (The women weren't allowed to make arrests.) Everyone agreed the raid was successful because of the exceptional sleuthing of Rhoda Milliken and the other policewomen.

Rhoda Milliken had been one of the new hires when the Washington, DC, Police Department made the unprecedented move to form a women's bureau within the organization in 1919. When Rhoda graduated from Barnard College in the class of 1918, she was unsure where her career would lead.

However, the American government major had completed many sociology courses and knew she wanted to do something in the "public interest" area. For a short time during the Great War, she worked as a civilian in the US Navy code service. Just as she was looking for another position, she heard about the formation of a women's division within the Washington, DC,

Metropolitan Police Department and decided to investigate the opportunities.

The qualifications were spelled out very clearly. Only well-educated women were considered. They were looking for women with four years of high school, some college, or work experience in social work or education. Recruits had to be at least 5 feet 4 inches tall, weigh no less than 115 pounds and no more than 170, and be between 25 and 35 years of age.

Women who wanted to join the new women's bureau were required to have "personality" and to have "sweet, wholesome faces"—on the order of the "classic beauty." However, the hiring director clarified that characteristic as "the beauty that comes from having a beautiful soul and desire to do some good in the world." They would be paid $1,460 per year.

Rhoda Milliken applied for a position and was offered a job. She fit the description. She was well educated and charming, and she possessed a delightful sense of humor. The fact that she had completed so many college credits in the sociology field made her especially appealing to the new director of the women's bureau as well.

The new agency was headed up by a woman named Mina Van Winkle, who had attended the New York School of Social Work and had worked as the director of a girls' reform school. She was a widow when she was hired to head the Washington, DC, Women's Bureau. After her marriage, Van Winkle had volunteered for years as a social worker, and she was the driving force behind the idea to run the new bureau using social-work principles.

The new bureau operated under the guidelines of the International Association of Policewomen. With the slogan "No woman is too good to be a policewoman," it was a group that advocated the formation of women's bureaus within police departments and saw their purpose as protective and preventive.

After being hired, Rhoda Milliken and the other recruits underwent a three-month training that included three hours per day of rigorous drilling in calisthenics and jujitsu. At the end of the training they would deal with cases in which women and children were involved either as offenders or victims. In addition, they would supplement the work of policemen.

The policewomen did not wear uniforms but wore street clothes, since it was a generally held belief that a distinction should be made between them and police*men*. Moreover, policewomen were considered less threatening and therefore more approachable to the women and children they were charged with protecting.

The policewomen were kept busy carrying out their work. One was always assigned to patrol Union Station in Washington—a major transportation hub with hundreds of trains coming and leaving every day. The policewoman was there to look for "willful girls" who used the lobby as a "recreational parlor" to meet travelers.

It was a time in the United States when some people thought morals were at an all-time low. City leaders claimed, "[It is a] well-known fact that boys and girls are becoming wayward and unmanageable at a younger age today than ever before." Many people—including Milliken—blamed the decline on a variety of factors. They believed the Great War (1914–1918) had contributed to the problem. Many parents—in the military or working in war industries—left children unattended at home for long periods of time each day.

Thousands of young women had moved to Washington to work in government jobs. At the same time, the city was overflowing with young soldiers and sailors. Automobiles also drew blame. Some called the car "the instrument of the devil." Young people engaged in "reckless automobile parties." Some cited films as contributing to the decline in young people, who could not resist the "lure of the movies."

At dance halls policewomen stepped in to stop "indecent dancing." They made sure the halls were well lighted in order to cut down on "spooning." At movie houses Milliken didn't hesitate to stop the reels at the hint of "indecent" or "dangerous" scenes. At the city's skating rinks policewomen walked through the skaters to prevent girls from making "undesirable and dangerous acquaintances."

Some of the policewomen were called "follow-up workers." They carried out duties associated with the aftermath of an apprehension of a girl or woman—helping to rehabilitate the offenders rather than incarcerating them. It was understood that probation and rehabilitation were more economical than incarceration since institutionalization of an offender cost an estimated $400 per person per year. (The cost per person in 2010 was over $31,000 per year.)

Rhoda Milliken quickly made a name for herself in the women's bureau. Whenever Director Van Winkle was away, Milliken was in charge. Soon she earned the title of *assistant director*. It didn't take long for her fellow officers to appreciate her easygoing manner and big heart. They affectionately called her simply "Milliken," and she liked that they felt comfortable around her. In 1921 she was promoted to sergeant—the first woman to reach the status in the Washington Police Department. With the exception of the director, she was the highest-ranking woman on the force. Now her coworkers called her "Sarge." In addition, Milliken's salary increased to $1,800 per year.

Throughout the 1930s Milliken and the women of the bureau continued the work they had been hired to do, but world events influenced the nature of their day-to-day challenges. During the years of the Great Depression (1929–1939) homelessness, unemployment, and alcoholism created problems for many people—and, in turn, more work for policewomen.

WHAT'S INDECENT?

Sometime before 1925 a law forbidding "indecent music" was put on the books in the city of Washington. It was quickly buried and forgotten before it got much attention. Then in the summer of 1925 it was unearthed, and city leaders decided it was time to start enforcing the law!

A debate ensued. How does one define "indecent music?" More than one city official tried, including policewoman Rhoda Milliken.

One official said this: "It's that tom-tommy sort of Oriental music that makes men forget home and babies."

And another: "You know what I mean, that hootchy-kootchy sort of intonation."

And Sergeant Milliken: "Any music played on a saxophone is immoral."

It's unclear if anyone was actually arrested for performing "indecent music." But more than one news story poked fun at the idea.

The *Washington Post* suggested that reformers should also give flowers their attention: after all, music affected only *one* of the senses, while roses "hit two of our senses at once—sight and smell," and "at times it makes one reel!" And how about those stars—those "little twinkling, saucy-hued eyes" that "lure us from the job"? "Reform astronomy too while we're at it!"

The women's bureau was charged with a new duty—solving missing persons' cases. At a time when many people wanted to walk away from their miserable lives, missing persons' cases were more frequent than ever—averaging six to eight reports per day in Washington. Many were young women and juvenile runaways.

By 1932 Rhoda Milliken had become the head of the bureau and had acquired the grade of captain, with a salary of $2,400 per year. Her background in sociology always led her to look for explanations for people's behavior, and her work with missing persons was no exception. "We find that there is usually something back of it all—trouble at home . . . difficulties at school," Rhoda said.

Rhoda was decades ahead of the times when she became an advocate for a national missing persons' bureau. She said such a network could house fingerprint records and photographs of missing persons. "This system would greatly aid police agencies throughout the country. It would be a simple matter to trace missing persons if something like this was handled properly," she asserted.

Alcoholism was a major problem, and the women's bureau was charged with handling any women who were arrested for intoxication. "It is a complicated and discouraging problem," Rhoda lamented. She was especially alarmed by the number of alcoholic women who had young children in their homes. She decried the fact that the district continued to deal with the problem by merely adding buildings to incarcerate people who were arrested for alcohol-related crimes. She wanted to see other solutions to the problem. In time, her wishes were realized when Washington adopted a system that allowed people arrested for alcohol violations to receive treatment at hospitals or clinics and to get help through Alcoholics Anonymous.

By the early 1940s new problems had replaced the difficulties of the Great Depression. Another war had broken out in
Europe, and America joined the fray in December 1941. Those
events led to a new assortment of issues for the women's bureau.

"If your daughter is emotionally unstable, keep her away
from wartime Washington," Captain Milliken warned parents.
Thousands of young girls were moving to the nation's capital to
take government jobs. Their average age was 20 years. At the
same time, thousands of young soldiers, sailors, and marines
were moving in and out of the city each day.

Those conditions led the director to add, "Parents who have
not bothered to instill character and responsibility in their
daughters are courting trouble by letting them come here." But
she also expected the military to take responsibility for their
actions. "It seems funny that everyone blames the teen-age
girls," she continued. She said military men of high rank were
often seen flirting with "all the bobby sox girls in sight." Rhoda
believed it was the women's bureau's duty to help all these
young men and women "tread the straight and narrow path."

In 1942 this "smiling, crinkly-eyed wisp of a cop" had a staff
of 23 experienced policewomen on her team. All were trained
social workers. In addition, she had 110 newly sworn-in volunteer police auxiliaries to do their part for the war effort. They
underwent 28 hours of training to learn the fundamentals of
evidence gathering, arrest procedures, and first aid.

Captain Milliken remarked on the upswing in shoplifting
in the war years. Always the social worker at heart, she looked
for causes for the criminal activity. She said the "nervous strain
of war" was partly responsible. "It's an emotional release," she
explained. "But it is a pretty costly cure for war nerves."

Another source of concern for law enforcement during the
1940s was a typical problem during wartime. Prostitution was

First aid class from the Washington, DC, Police Department.
Library of Congress, LC-USZ62-116712

on the rise; and because it was considered a "women's issue," it became a women's bureau issue. However, Rhoda Milliken approached the problem from a perspective that was unusual for the time. She believed the emphasis should be on fighting prostitution "as an accepted part of community life"—and not "against the prostitute alone." She said law enforcement and society in general were concerned with the "persecution of individual women" while discounting the "great network of which their activities are a part."

Throughout the early 1940s Rhoda and her women's bureau continued to struggle with issues related to youthful offenders—or juvenile delinquents. She said it was her "biggest headache." She saw a rise in delinquency by 32 percent between 1940 and 1942. Captain Milliken looked beyond the statistics and sought out possible causes. She always looked to the family for issues that caused distress for children.

Again Rhoda Milliken was ahead of her time. She said there was nothing new in her assertion that quarrels, drunkenness, cruelty, and insecurity in families led children to lives of crime. However, she said people needed to be reminded of this because "we never really do much about it." According to her, youthful offenders often end up as adult offenders—causing the corrections systems immense amounts of money. She saw a solution in prevention, and she was hopeful. "Maybe we will spend more money on prevention instead of at the other end of the problem," she predicted.

By 1945 Rhoda said the district was "holding the line" against juvenile delinquency. She reported that juvenile arrests had

A chief duty of Washington, DC, policewomen was managing delinquents.
Library of Congress LC-USZ62-116713

leveled off to "about 3,600 per year." She credited a concerted effort of cooperation among community groups—police, city officials, churches, and parents. She said all worked together to "keep youth healthy, happy, and constructively busy."

Milliken had become a nationally known expert in the field of juvenile crime. She spoke to civic groups in other cities touting the success she had seen in Washington. She credited neighborhood councils working to help kids find healthy leisure activities. Police department Boys and Girls Clubs were also part of the solution. "The best thing the police-sponsored clubs have done is to change the children's attitude toward law enforcement officers. A child who considers himself the policeman's friend is not likely to cross swords with him," Rhoda explained.

When Rhoda talked about the role of women's bureaus in other cities, she humorously remarked that generally police departments pushed off on women's divisions "all the things that embarrass their brother officers and make them feel uncomfortable—runaway children, runaway husbands, sex offenders."

When the Washington, DC, Women's Bureau hired its first policewomen in 1919, beautiful women were encouraged to apply. Beauty was defined as a characteristic that "comes from having a beautiful soul and desire to do some good in the world." Rhoda Milliken was hired because she had completed many sociology courses in her college work. But after over 30 years in police work in the district, it was obvious that she was also a beautiful person.

When asked in an interview about her resilience as a policewoman, Rhoda Milliken replied, "with a sparkle in her eye," "In this job you have to smile. It's either sink or swim."

LEARN MORE

International Association of Women Police
www.iawp.org

US Department of Justice, National Missing and
Unidentified Persons System
www.namus.gov

Washington, DC, Metropolitan Police Department
http://mpdc.dc.gov

PENNY HARRINGTON

........·······

A Relentless Pioneer

"FAT, HOMELY, DOUBLE-CHIN humpback cow."

"A freak like you."

Penny Harrington overcame both overt sexist remarks such as these from her fellow officers and her bosses' covert maneuvering, to become the first female police chief of a major US city. She used determination and the legal system to tackle obstacles she faced in the male-dominated world of policing in the 1960s through the mid-1980s.

Nurse, teacher, or secretary—as a young girl growing up in Michigan in the 1950s and '60s, Penny Harrington knew there were only limited career choices open to her. There were women in other professions, but they were exceptions. And, as Penny would learn, women who chose to break traditions faced immense barriers.

When Penny was in high school, she heard about an opportunity to get out of school for a day. The school was offering a career day—giving students a chance to shadow a career professional. Penny jumped at the chance and was paired up with a woman who worked in law enforcement. This day changed her life forever.

After graduation from high school, Penny enrolled at Michigan State University and majored in police administration. It was here that she first faced sexism in the law enforcement world. Male students were tracked into classes dealing with crime scene investigations, evidence gathering, and fingerprinting—all skills they would use as police*men*. Females were steered toward child psychology and juvenile justice classes— areas they would eventually work in as police*women*.

It was a time before men and women who worked in law enforcement were known as police *officers*. There were good reasons for differentiating with distinct titles. Policemen were very different from policewomen—in terms of duties, pay scales, and opportunities for advancement.

After completing her coursework at the university, Penny was hired by the Portland, Oregon, Police Department. It was 1964, and she was one of only 18 women on the 700-member force. She was assigned to the Women's Protective Division— the only division open to

Penny Harrington.
City of Portland Archives, Oregon,
A2000-026.39

women. Penny and the other policewomen wore white gloves, hats, tailored suits with silk blouses, and slingback pumps, and they carried purses. But clothing wasn't the only difference between the policewomen and policemen.

For women to be considered for employment as policewomen in Portland, they had to have a college education. Men were required to have only a high school education or a GED (general educational development). In addition, all policewomen were paid less than policemen.

Policewomen handled any crimes associated with children—abuse, neglect, and runaways. They also were in charge of sex abuse, prostitution, and rape cases. Penny soon became the "expert" in the division that handled child abuse cases. It wasn't something she enjoyed, but no one else wanted to deal with these heartbreaking cases. Child abuse was difficult to prove, and victims were often placed back in their home situations. After five years Penny was ready for a change. She was burnt out after seeing children injured and killed at the hands of parents or other adults.

Unfortunately, the Portland Police Department had a policy that prevented Penny from changing jobs. All policewomen worked in the Women's Protective Division. They weren't allowed to work in or apply for police positions outside their division. So Penny was stuck—along with the other policewomen in the Portland Police Department.

Late in 1969 Penny learned of a position in the new Planning and Research Division of the department. It was established to help improve the function of the police department, and Penny wanted to be part of it. Despite the policy that prevented women from transferring out of the women's division, the director of Planning and Research encouraged Penny to apply. After completing an exam and interview, the director offered Penny the job. At last she would leave her grueling responsibilities in the women's division.

"Over my dead body," was the response of the chief of police when he heard one of his policewomen was leaving the Women's Protective Division to transfer into another division within the department. No woman had done it in the past, and Penny Harrington would not do it now!

The mayor of Portland appointed the chief of police, so Penny decided to take her fight to the top. She went to the mayor's office and demanded to see him. When she entered his office and told him about her frustrations with the police department policies, the mayor said he couldn't do anything about it, to which Penny replied, "What do you mean there's nothing you can do? I'm going to sue you!"

By the time she returned to the police department, she received word that she would indeed be allowed to transfer to the Planning and Research Division! The threat of a lawsuit changed the mayor's and the chief's minds about Penny's transfer out of the women's division. It was a first—one of many for Penny.

After this experience Penny began to realize that a simple seven-letter word was preventing her and other Portland policewomen from applying for positions and qualifying for promotions. When a position opened outside the women's division, the qualifications were always clearly listed: "patrolmen." Women were *policewomen*, not *patrolmen*. A simple solution to the problem, as Penny saw it, was to refer to all as police *officers*.

She put in a written request to have everyone in the police bureau reclassified as police *officers*, a request that the Civil Service Board and the newly elected female mayor approved. Penny and her fellow female officers knew how important the new classification was for them, but no one else seemed to pay much attention to a change that seemed trivial.

In the spring of 1971 a detective position opened up in the police department, and now the "who may apply" section listed "police officers." Penny and four other women applied. Penny had the highest score among the women and ranked fourth overall. The top three on the list—all men—were promoted to detective status immediately. Then, promotions stopped. No explanation was offered.

Finally, almost a year after hitting the top of the list, Penny was promoted to detective. Penny was the first female detective in the Portland Police Department. She was excited to meet her new challenges. She knew that she would face dangerous situations, but she was prepared. She knew how to use a gun and had a brown belt in jujitsu. Despite this, the chief of police was not happy about having a female detective in his department. As he handed Penny her new badge, he said in a soft voice that only she could hear, "Don't you come complaining to me if you get shot."

Penny continued to move through the ranks of the police department. She applied for and was promoted to sergeant, lieutenant, and captain. In each case, Penny was the first female to hold the position. In her job interviews she was asked questions that men were not asked: "What will you do for a babysitter?" "What if male officers' wives are jealous of you?" Also, in each case, Penny's promotion was held up for unexplained reasons. Sometimes hiring stopped just as Penny hit the top of the list. Other times the list was allowed to expire as her name hit the top. Sometimes there were no positions available.

Penny was patient and resolute at times. At other times she was impatient but determined. Sometimes she used the law to help. She filed 42 complaints for sex discrimination with the civil service board between 1973 and 1978. Most had to do with pay and education discrepancies between males and females. One had to do with the height requirement, which discriminated against women, who were generally smaller in stature. Penny and other women in the division conducted research showing that height had no relation to the agility of police officers. Many other law enforcement agencies around the country—including the National Park Service—had stopped their height requirements. The women were successful in convincing the Portland Police Department to discontinue the unfair practice.

In late 1979 when Penny's name hit the top of the eligibility list for a captain's position, there were no openings. So she had an idea that would create one. She had noticed that officers were engaging in some questionable activities during the afternoon and night shifts—when most of the command staff was off duty. Penny wrote a proposal to add a night commander. In addition, morale was low, the force needed officers with diverse ethnic backgrounds, and discipline was haphazard. Penny convinced the chief that a captain of personnel could work on improving the weaknesses. The chief agreed to Penny's ideas and gave her the position, promoting her to captain!

As the youngest and first female captain in the department, Penny was determined to make a difference. Her priority was to recruit more women and people of color. She called upon community leaders to help. She went to churches, social service agencies, and business owners to get their input. She trained personnel officers to be sensitive to diverse cultures. She changed the location of the police exams so they were more accessible. Under her direction the department offered classes to help potential recruits pass civil service exams.

Penny began to make an impression on the community, and people took notice of their first female police captain. Many believed she was doing a great job, and some began mentioning her name as a possible chief of police candidate when a new mayor would take office in 1985.

When a man named Bud Clark ran for mayor of Portland in 1984, voters loved him. His slogan was "This Bud's for you," and he passed out rosebuds on street corners. He was elected and took office in early 1985.

Shortly after, the chief of police position opened up, and Penny was one of 14 who applied. A panel interviewed the candidates, whittling the list to 4, one of whom was Penny Harrington—the only woman.

Penny knew in her heart that she would get the job, and she was prepared to hit the ground running. When the new mayor announced his decision, Penny was not disappointed. The new chief of police of Portland, Penny Harrington, was the first female chief among the nation's 40 largest cities. All the major news agencies, television networks, and magazines were abuzz. Penny was a celebrity.

Penny identified three main goals she hoped to accomplish as soon as possible: (1) put more officers on the streets, (2) connect with the community, and (3) get tough on juvenile crime. But before she could begin, the mayor hit her with a major obstacle. He ordered her to cut her budget by 10 percent!

Despite the setback from budget cuts, Penny forged ahead with her plans. She reorganized the narcotics division, which had been riddled with scandal—officers planting drugs and taking money off suspects. She also wanted more supervision of the officers who worked in the division, which caused a jolt to the force. Members of the narcotics division were up in arms and let Penny and the public know about their discontent. They filed complaints with the union. More and more of her decisions rankled the union membership, and before long she was described by the union president as "lousy."

To adapt to the budget cuts, Penny had to cut 72 of 963 officers' jobs. This also caused discontent among the officers. But she persevered. She made a very unpopular choice about the horse patrol. It was eating up far too much of the tight budget—$500,000 per year. The horses held a soft spot in the hearts of citizens of Portland and the officers who patrolled on horseback. When Penny refused to change her decision to eliminate the special patrol, a private citizens' group raised the money to keep it in operation.

Penny kept her word and set up a special juvenile division and truancy program. She knew from her years on the force that daytime burglaries were usually the result of truants—kids who should have been in school. To combat the problem, Penny assigned officers to patrol outside the city's schools. They stopped kids on the streets and contacted school personnel as well as parents. They connected truants to social agencies and school programs that provided assistance and training.

DON'T CHOKE 'EM; SMOKE 'EM. This slogan was printed on T-shirts that some Portland police officers were selling in April 1985, and the words ignited strong reaction in the city's black community. ("Smoke 'em" was police slang for "shoot them.") The phrase referred to an incident that occurred between white officers and an unarmed African American man who was killed as a result of a restraining hold the police administered. The man's death and the T-shirts led to accusations of racism within the police department and to headaches and heartache for the chief of police.

On a Sunday evening late in April 1985, Lloyd Stevenson, a 31-year-old off-duty security guard with five kids and no criminal record, got in the midst of a fray at a convenience store parking lot. Police had been called to a robbery taking place in the store, and Lloyd was in a crowd that had gathered outside. He and another fellow started fighting when the man directed a racial slur at Lloyd. The officers who were responding to the robbery saw the two fighting and rushed to intervene.

One of the officers applied the carotid hold to Lloyd. An approved maneuver for officers at the time, it was supposed to cause the victim to faint. However, something went wrong, and Lloyd stopped breathing. Although police summoned an ambulance, he was pronounced dead at the hospital.

Police Chief Harrington was notified of the situation and took immediate action. After learning the facts, she said she believed the officers had conducted themselves in an appropriate manner. The hold was an approved method of restraint in the Portland Police Department.

Many in the community, including some African American leaders, were outraged that an unarmed man had died at the hands of the police. Penny spoke to key people in the black community and assured them that a thorough investigation would occur. She told the officers that they had followed approved procedures in using the carotid hold. However, she put a temporary ban on future use of the maneuver. She wanted to learn more about it and other options available to officers in subduing victims.

Protestors took to the streets, marching outside Penny's office. Some held signs that read BAN THE HOLD, STOP THE KILLING. They wanted the carotid hold banned permanently, and they wanted the police who used it on Lloyd Stevenson to be fired and charges brought.

The union attacked the chief for banning the hold. Union leaders said it was a valuable tool for officers and that the chief was endangering officers' lives with the ban. They reminded her and the public that it had been an approved form of restraint for more than 10 years in Portland.

On the day of Lloyd Stevenson's funeral, Penny heard that two police officers were selling T-shirts emblazoned with the offensive "smoke 'em" slogan. She was angry that members of the force could be so thoughtless and malicious. She learned the identities of the men and suspended them. After she learned more, she decided to fire them. "I cannot have those men on the police bureau because of their poor judgment and their total disregard for the community," she said.

Eventually a grand jury was called to investigate the death of Lloyd Stevenson. When the officers were exonerated, the union lauded the decision. The African American community was stunned. In addition, a labor arbitrator reinstated the two officers whom Penny had fired over the T-shirt incident.

It was at this time that Penny was subjected to the most vicious attacks. She believed many of the anonymous messages came from within the department. She also received death threats and soon had a bodyguard who went everywhere with her.

Controversy continued to plague Penny. Police killed two African American citizens—one an elderly grandmother whom they mistook for a criminal. Penny was also widely unpopular among her subordinates. In a survey of police officers, 91 percent of the respondents rated her performance as "poor" or "below average." In March 1986 the mayor formed a commission to investigate and report on a variety of issues surrounding his chief. The commission investigated (and exonerated) her officer husband for misconduct in a drug investigation. They questioned Penny's decision to reorganize the drug division early in her tenure. In the end the commission criticized her management style and recommended her dismissal.

Only 17 months after becoming the first female police chief of a major US city, Penny was out of a job. The entire nation had watched her rise; now it witnessed her departure—under sensational circumstances. News headlines blasted the story across the country: UNDER FIRE, WOMAN QUITS AS PORTLAND POLICE

CHIEF and FIRST WOMAN TO HEAD BIG-CITY POLICE DEPARTMENT RESIGNS. *Time* magazine described her as a "tarnished penny."

Penny never worked as a police officer again. She took a position with the California State Bar Association handling citizen complaints against the state's lawyers and overseeing training among investigative units. Later she started a consulting business through which she offered counseling in discrimination and sexual harassment cases.

Penny compared her time as chief to "a ride on a bucking bronco." Although her short tenure as chief of police was a rocky ride professionally and personally, it culminated her decades-long career as a relentless pioneer for women in law enforcement. Because of Penny's tenacity, determination, and courage, she shattered barriers for women who wanted equality in the male-dominated world of law enforcement. Other police departments, such as those in Houston, Texas, and Atlanta, Georgia, soon followed suit and appointed women as chiefs.

LEARN MORE

Let Me Play: The Story of Title IX: The Law That Changed the Future of Girls in America by Karen Blumenthal (Atheneum Books for Young Readers, 2005)

"Mounted Patrol Unit," Police Bureau, City of Portland, Oregon
www.portlandoregon.gov/police/article/250328

Triumph of Spirit: An Autobiography by Chief Penny Harrington by Penny Harrington (Brittany, 1999)

JODY KASPER

An Impassable Woman

"I WAS AN OK STUDENT. I didn't actually know if I could make it in college," recalled Jody Kasper, chief of police in Northampton, Massachusetts.

Jody not only made it in college—she earned a bachelor's and two master's degrees on her way to the top law enforcement position in the city.

The 40-year-old started school when she was only 4 years old and overcame a speech problem that required a couple years of therapy before her teachers and other students could understand her. ("My mom and sister had to decode for me!" Jody says.) An athletic kid who loved to ride bikes, swim, and build forts, she was the only girl on the Little League team and was the pitcher. One of her favorite toys was her Lego set. But Jody refused to limit her creations to the models; she mixed all the sets together and built "giant structures like Ferris wheels and roller coasters."

Jody's determination to overcome her speech challenges, stand out as the only girl on an all-male team, and go beyond the limits in Lego building were early examples of her ability to excel while making history. In 2015 the City of Northampton chose Jody to lead its law enforcement agency—the first time a woman held the post. She became a member of an elite group—only 1 percent of police chiefs in the nation were women in 2015.

Jody's journey to the top post was a result of her hard work and tenacity, certainly; however, she credits a high school educator with being the catalyst that propelled her down her career path. One day during a visit to her high school guidance office, the counselor handed Jody a community college course catalog. "Pick out what's interesting to you," she said. "I gravitated toward the law enforcement classes," Jody remarked.

And the rest is history. After completing community college, Jody earned a bachelor's degree in criminal justice and psychology. She later earned a master of science in criminal justice and a master's degree in public administration. But those advanced degrees came after she had a few years of actual policing under her belt.

The Northampton Police Department hired Jody fresh out of Westfield State University. After completing the 21-week-long municipal police academy, she hit the streets as an officer. Her first assignment was "walking a beat" on the 11 PM to 7 AM shift. It was a typical assignment for rookie cops—but not a coveted one. And although she says there was a "lot of activity in the dark" for her to investigate, after a year on the job Jody was eager to move on from the night duty. When she saw an opportunity to spend time on the job doing just what she loved to do as a kid—ride a bike—she went for it!

As a bicycle patrol officer, Jody took advantage of her position to build relationships within her community. She knew how important it was for the citizens of Northampton to see their police officers as members of their community—there to protect and serve. It was also an especially busy assignment that gave her the opportunity to handle a large number of calls each shift.

Jody also patrolled the city streets from her patrol car. About half her time was spent responding to calls—complaints about loud neighbors, medical emergencies, accidents, and criminal activities. The other half was officer initiated—routine car stops, issuing tickets, drug searches, and serving warrants.

Almost every cop movie or police drama on television includes a chase scene, and Jody experienced this in real life. One New Year's Eve she was working the overnight shift. While in the downtown area of the city, she got a call for assistance from a fellow officer. As the officer and Jody pursued the suspect on foot, the other officer lost sight of him. Then Jody spotted him in a neighborhood. For a quarter mile she ran after the suspect—through backyards and over fences—all the while

Jody Kasper on patrol.
Courtesy of Jody Kasper

using her flashlight to light her way. Finally she caught him in a meadow area and, with the other officer, took him into custody.

In another instance Jody was again working the midnight shift when she performed a routine car stop. She noticed the driver seemed very anxious as she began to question him. Suddenly he sped off—running over the front of Jody's boot! She notified dispatch of her pursuit and "gave chase." At one point the driver turned down a dead-end street and ended up crashing at the end of the roadway. Jody ordered him from the car and held him at gunpoint. When backup arrived, Jody and a fellow officer arrested the man. Had the suspect not fled, his only charges would have been driving with a suspended license. However, because he took off, he faced a variety of additional charges!

After three years as a patrol officer, Jody applied to be promoted to detective and got the promotion. "Detectives get a lot of interesting cases—some really crazy stuff," Jody says. "You get to knock down doors sometimes."

As was often the case with female detectives, she handled cases related to child abuse, sexual assault, and family crimes. The practice was a holdover from the early days of law enforcement when women officers were expected to fulfill the role of social workers.

"I certainly have noticed differences in male and female officers over the years," Jody said in a 2009 interview. "These differences have little to do with actual police work on the street and more to do with the differences in the way women are perceived by male officers and how women perceive themselves."

As a detective, Jody wore plain clothes and was on call 24 hours a day. She was called to crime scenes and death investigations. She was required to perform specialized duties that she learned on the job and in special courses designed to provide detectives with valuable skills—courses such as advanced detective school, homicide investigation, and interview and interrogation. She learned practical techniques like detecting physical evidence at crime scenes. Jody recalls one especially interesting case that required her to use some of those skills.

She and a partner were called to a break-in at a Northampton building that housed three separate businesses. Arriving at the scene, Jody, her partner, and a crime scene technician found plenty of evidence the suspect left behind. They were able to discern a fingerprint left on the point of entry—a window. Inside they saw a door between two of the businesses that someone had pried open with tools. The team spotted shoe prints that revealed unusual patterns on the soles.

They spent the day working the case. A visit to a shoe store helped them identify the brand and style of shoe the suspect wore, based on the unique impressions left at the scene. As Jody and her partner canvassed the neighborhood to gather more information, they decided to visit the occupant of the apartment over the burglarized businesses. Stepping off the elevator, they could see shoe prints leading to the apartment—prints that bore the unusual patterns they had seen at the scene!

After securing a warrant, Jody and her partner entered the apartment and found the tools that had been used in the burglary. Although he had discarded his shoes in a dumpster and the detectives were never able to locate them, they did obtain a photo of the suspect wearing shoes identical to the ones with the unusual patterns; and he was eventually arrested for the crime. "It was good police work—and good luck!" Jody says.

Jody remained a detective for five years. As she began to move up the ranks within the department, she assumed administrative duties. This meant she supervised other officers and oversaw various new initiatives. In 2007 she became a patrol staff sergeant, and in 2011 a patrol lieutenant. As a staff sergeant she was responsible for the proficiency, discipline, conduct, and appearance of all the officers on her shift. She continued to respond to calls with fellow officers; but she was also responsible for providing direction on crime scenes, conducting internal investigations, and evaluating officer performance. As lieutenant she was a shift commander of 15 officers and 2 sergeants. She handled citizen complaints, oversaw processing and detention of suspects, and evaluated staff performance.

One of the initiatives Jody developed as patrol lieutenant was training to deal with individuals who exhibit a condition called "excited delirium." It's a state "usually with people under the influence of drugs," Jody explains. "They're freaking out, are dangerous, and often combative."

Jody recalls an incident in which she was called to handle a man in a city park who showed signs of excited delirium. "He was punching people, and it was as though he was looking through you. He showed an insane amount of strength." She says two officers were injured attempting to take the man to the ground. While it was important for police to arrest the man, Jody emphasized that he was undergoing a medical crisis and it was most important to get him to a hospital.

In 2013 Jody became a detective lieutenant and assumed command of all detective bureau operations, including overseeing all felony and misdemeanor cases, assigning cases to staff, and directing crime scenes and drug forfeitures.

By 2014 she had become captain of operations and supervised all patrol division and detective bureau operations—overseeing the work of 65 personnel. She was in charge of hiring and promoting staff, and managed internal affairs investigations. In an attempt to improve morale, she implemented an employee climate survey that assessed ways to change unsatisfactory practices. She also introduced an employee evaluation policy and an exit interview process. To improve physical strength and stamina and job readiness for employees, she offered a fitness program that included optional annual fitness tests. In response to community concerns about quality of life issues in the downtown area of Northampton, Jody required officers to engage in foot patrol for a portion of their shifts.

Jody's day-to-day activities included dealing with the usual police calls—disturbances, drunk drivers, and burglaries. There was the time a car dealership called police to investigate when three dozen cars had been broken into. It wasn't a typical burglary—no cars were stolen. "Every once in a while, we've had incidents where rims are taken off of a car, tires, but we haven't seen anything to this level in a long time," Jody said at the time. She was referring to the stealing of air bags from the cars! "We found about 36 vehicles that had been broken into," Jody said. "Windows were smashed and airbags were removed from the steering columns."

And there was the case where a man lost his temper at a pizzeria and ended up with charges of assault and battery brought against him. The 24-year-old seemed to think a 30-minute wait for his food was out of line. The suspect "felt that it took too long. He said that he was out of here, that he wanted his money back," Jody explained to the local media. The pizzeria employees refunded the money and gave him his pizza, but he still wasn't satisfied. He said they threw the items at him, and he responded by knocking over a cash register as he made his way behind the counter. Then he spotted another customer videotaping the incident, and he grabbed the guy's phone, smashing it on the ground. He picked up a vintage gumball machine and tossed it at an employee, hitting him in the leg. By now the police had arrived and arrested the suspect.

All in a day's work for Jody and her fellow officers!

In June 2015 Jody Kasper made history by becoming the first female chief of police in Northampton, dutifully reciting the oath of service: "I, Jody D. Kasper, do solemnly swear to faithfully and impartially discharge the duties of chief of police in the Northampton Police Department in accordance with the rules and policies of the police department, the ordinances of the city of Northampton, and the constitution of this commonwealth, to the best of my knowledge and ability."

From a field of 34 candidates from across the country, the mayor named Jody to the position, and the city council unanimously approved the choice after a rigorous interview process.

"I've never paid much attention to my gender as I've moved through my career," Jody remarked. "I came in each day and worked very hard. I've put in for opportunities when they were presented and was selected for promotions when I earned them."

Jody's colleague, Capt. John Cartledge says, "She understands the importance of building relationships with people in our community. She knows that getting to know our citizens and providing them opportunities to know us will help us all work better together to solve problems." As chief, Jody is the final authority on all matters of policy, operations, and discipline. Shortly after moving into her new position, Jody collaborated with police union leaders to improve the existing policy on promotions among the staff. And she implemented a software program that more fairly assigns work duties to officers. Additionally, she has brought back a student resource officer (SRO) to the school district after a two-year absence.

"The SRO isn't just there for criminal investigations, but also to help kids and mentor them. Sometimes kids need a little guidance," Jody said.

Jody continues to look for ways to recruit women to police work—as she has throughout her career. She says women are less likely than men to consider careers in law enforcement, for a number of reasons: they have not typically seen women in those careers, they have not seen female family members enter law enforcement careers, and they seldom see women in leadership roles in police departments. Under Jody's direction the Northampton Police Department's website underwent a redesign, showing more women in police roles. And the department has begun recruiting at two local women's colleges.

The new chief is a proponent of community policing. She has said the term *law enforcement* is too narrow, because police work involves much more than enforcing the law. She said police *do* enforce laws but that progressive police agencies use "expanded strategies" to "enhance public safety." They collaborate with other community agencies to improve the quality of life for citizens, emphasize education, and focus on crime prevention.

"I've always been a huge believer in community policing," Jody said. "If we have good relationships with each other, it's easier to share information and prevent rumors and false information from spreading."

Jody has admitted that the city of Northampton is a special community in many ways. "I am incredibly fortunate to work in a progressive community that emphasizes equality and social justice."

While Jody faced sexism on the job at different times in her professional life, she says she didn't let those occasions overshadow her career. And she has said that women in law enforcement careers are constantly working to prove themselves on the job. "I believe that as women we are constantly challenged to do more and do better in a career-long effort to prove ourselves." She tells other women interested in law enforcement to make themselves "impassable"—so outstanding that it's impossible to pass over them when looking for individuals to fill leadership roles.

Jody Kasper, Chief of Police.
Courtesy of Jody Kasper

Realizing that, Jody made every effort to "do more" and "do better" as she moved through her career—making herself impassable to the mayor and city council of Northampton. How many of the other candidates applying for the chief's position had a bachelor's degree, two master's degrees, college teaching experience, and had authored numerous articles and books on law enforcement—as Jody has? A very impassable individual!

While Jody recognizes her own hard work and accomplishments as a police professional, she has also gives credit to other women who paved the way for her: "I don't want to brush over being a female chief. I want to recognize that it is unique and that it's an opportunity I have only because of the many women who have led the way. It is thanks to them that my gender has not been a consideration of mine as I have moved through my career."

Jody reminds people, however, that police officers make tremendous sacrifices as they carry out their duties. "We have missed our children's bedtimes, birthdays, band concerts, and soccer games. We have missed family holidays and special events. This job is not easy," Jody said. While Jody's family has made sacrifices for her career, they are also proud of her.

"I admire Jody for taking on such an important job and for her thoughtful and confident approach to leadership and policing. And I am proud that she is a role model for other young people who are interested in the career," says Melissa, Jody's partner.

One of those young people is Jody's 11-year-old son, Jackson.

"It's really neat to be able to tell people that your mom is the chief of police," he says.

LEARN MORE

"Swearing in of Northampton Chief of Police Jody Kasper," YouTube video, July 1, 2015
www.youtube.com/watch?v=peUnCupTWQU

"10 Rookie Errors to Avoid" by Jody Kasper, *Police: The Law Enforcement Magazine*, May 18, 2010
www.policemag.com/channel/careers-training
/articles/2010/05/10-rookie-errors-to-avoid.aspx

PART V

GETTING INTO GOVERNMENT

Federal Agents

AUSTRIAN IMMIGRANTS arriving in the port of New Orleans on the *Sofia Hohenberg* in September 1907 were surprised to be met by an American woman who said she represented the US attorney general, Charles Joseph Bonaparte (grandnephew of Napoleon Bonaparte). Mary G. Quackenbos was an attorney—"the only woman employed by the US Secret Service"—according to a newspaper at the time. She was looking for passengers whom local lumber camps and sawmills in the South were bringing in. It was common for these industries to use immigrants for labor—paying their passage but forcing the immigrants to work until their debts were paid. It was a practice known as peonage, and it was illegal.

In the early 1900s the Department of Treasury also hired women to board ships arriving in the nation's ports. These women searched female passengers who were trying to avoid paying duties on imported objects such as lace and silks. However, one female customs inspector complained that she wasn't busy enough now that women's styles had moved away from hooped skirts and layers of petticoats—fashions used by devious women to hide their smuggled goods.

While the federal government was known to hire women for special law enforcement assignments in the early 1900s, it didn't happen on a wide-scale basis; and it was the exception to the norm. In fact, it would be over 70 years before the two major federal law enforcement agencies allowed women in positions as anything other than clerical workers; and it took federal legislation to precipitate it.

In 1969 President Richard Nixon issued Executive Order 11478, which stated that the federal government could not use gender as a qualification for hiring. Less than two years later the Supreme Court ruled that the equal protection clause in the 14th Amendment of the US Constitution prohibited discrimination on the basis of sex. Soon after, the Secret Service and the Federal Bureau of Investigation hired their first female agents. It was a turning point for women in federal law enforcement.

Just because there were laws in place, it didn't mean being the firsts in these positions would be easy. But because of the determination and courage of many women who came first, those who followed faced less rocky roads. The pioneers opened the way for many women to consider and pursue fulfilling careers in law enforcement.

ROSANNE RUSSO

....

Using Psychology to Catch Criminals

SHE HAD BEEN STABBED and left to die at the bottom of the stairs outside her basement apartment, a 57-year-old widow who lived alone and whom neighbors described as likeable and friendly. She was often seen walking her dogs in a neighborhood of an Upstate New York city—those dogs might have fought off her attacker if they hadn't been shut up in the apartment. A friend discovered the body after becoming concerned when she couldn't reach the woman. By that time, the woman had been dead four days.

The local police secured the crime scene and started their investigation. Then they decided to call in the Federal Bureau of Investigation (FBI). It wasn't unusual for metropolitan police departments to ask for assistance from the FBI to develop a profile of a suspect. However, it was noteworthy for the agency to assign a female agent—fresh out of criminal profiling training—to tackle the case.

Rosanne Russo, with exactly two years in the FBI and only three months out of specialized profile training, took on this, her first profiling case, in 1982. She pulled from her background as a school psychologist—along with her FBI Academy training—to develop a physical and psychological description of the individual who had murdered the woman.

She met with the local police detectives to learn details of the homicide, visited the crime scene, and viewed evidence. Rosanne wanted to know everything she could about the victim. She pored over photos of the crime scene, read the autopsy report, and interviewed the medical examiner to glean more from his investigation.

The victim was heavyset and had medical problems; she could not move very quickly. She had been stabbed multiple times with three different weapons—all left at the scene. The body had not been moved. Her hands bore numerous wounds, indicating she had defended herself.

From Rosanne's observations, she developed a profile of the suspect: a black male, age 16 to 21, living within walking distance of the crime. He may have lived with his parents, was unemployed, had average or less-than-average intelligence, and had not completed high school. He may have been arrested in the past for disorderly conduct or crimes against a person, but he had not previously committed a homicide. He was an angry, impulsive, and disorganized individual with an unkempt appearance.

Within a few months a 20-year-old black man who lived in the neighborhood was arrested. He lived with his older brother, had not completed high school, had less-than-average intelligence, and was a known drug user. He had been arrested previously for possession of weapons, and had a scruffy appearance.

The local authorities and Rosanne's supervisors at the FBI were very impressed by how closely the suspect paralleled the profile she had put together. And Rosanne was more convinced than ever that she had made the right career choice when she left a Wisconsin school district to pursue a career in the FBI.

Sunday nights at the Russo household in Sheboygan, Wisconsin, in 1965 found 13-year-old Rosanne glued to the television set watching actor Efrem Zimbalist Jr. solve baffling criminal cases on the popular series *The FBI*. Rosanne was drawn to the fictional cases because they allowed her to exercise her skills as a problem solver; however, she could only fantasize about working for the FBI, because females were not allowed in the agency until 1972.

Rosanne also loved reading the Nancy Drew mystery series that was popular at the time. Nancy was a fictional girl detective—someone with whom Rosanne could identify—who put her inquisitive nature to work solving crimes. Although Rosanne didn't actually know any female detectives, Nancy Drew gave her confidence that anything was possible. And it spurred her desire for a career that involved travel and adventure.

When Rosanne entered college at the University of Wisconsin in the fall of 1970, she aspired to a career as an airline flight attendant (or "stewardess"). She knew it would give her the opportunity to travel and see the world. And there were very few occupations open to women that offered exciting endeavors and intriguing ventures. But an airline industry job was not in Rosanne's future.

By the time Rosanne had completed her first year at college, she had been introduced to the study of human behavior, and she committed to a major in psychology. It was a perfect choice for someone who liked to pose hypotheses, design studies, collect data, interpret results, and solve problems.

After earning a master's degree in school psychology, Rosanne took a job in Racine County, Wisconsin, where for nearly four years she enjoyed a career as school psychologist.

But she began to crave more diversity and different challenges, and wanted to fulfill her longstanding desire for adventure and travel.

"I had an overpowering feeling there was something else I needed to do," Rosanne says.

The "something else" presented itself when Rosanne heard that the FBI was interested in hiring psychologists. After completing an application, she took a written test that included vocabulary, reading, writing, and spelling. It also consisted of a psychological and personality inventory that required the applicants to explain how they would react in specific situations. Next Rosanne participated in an interview, and finally a physical exam. She passed all the steps to become an agent and within a few months entered the FBI training at the headquarters in Quantico, Virginia.

Rosanne had never shot or held a weapon, but that changed very quickly the day she began her 16-week schooling to become an agent—one of 11 women in a class of 33. The firearms portion was only one part of the school, but it was a significant part. No one could become an agent unless he or she could handle and qualify with a revolver and shotgun.

The firearms training took place at an outdoor range in the very cold Virginia winter. Rosanne found it challenging—her fingers were stiff from the cold as she tried to load bullets. All the while the instructors were yelling, reminding the students that the minutes were ticking by in the timed tests. Some students felt intimidated by the shouting instructors, all but one of whom were male. And some instructors disapproved of the idea of women as FBI agents.

Rosanne and her fellow students at the academy spent much of their time in a classroom learning legal issues. The FBI legal experts held classes to help them understand the agency's jurisdiction for enforcing federal criminal laws, investigating threats to national security, and assisting other law enforcement agencies.

In addition, the training included learning how to utilize investigative tools, such as interviewing techniques, developing informants, and collecting evidence. Students also learned investigative procedures such as the polygraph, fingerprinting, handwriting comparison, and blood sample analysis.

And last, physical training was part of the course. There was running, climbing ropes and walls, repelling, swimming, jumping from a high dive, and maneuvering through an outdoor obstacle course. They were required to complete 35 push-ups, 35 pull-ups, and 50 sit-ups. And to aid them in the event of resistance during an arrest, they practiced defensive tactics such as boxing and wrestling.

Doing qualifying pull-ups at FBI training.
Courtesy of Rosanne Russo

Women in Rosanne's FBI graduating class. Rosanne is in the back row, second from right.
Courtesy of Rosanne Russo

By March 1980 Rosanne had completed all the requirements and graduated from the FBI Academy. She was off and running in her new career, which would eventually span over 28 years. As she made her way to her first assignment as an agent in the Milwaukee, Wisconsin, field office, she was excited and eager. She was about to embark on a journey that would fulfill her desire for travel and adventure—just as she had anticipated. But she had no idea that she also would make FBI history by becoming the agency's first female profiler.

Rosanne spent nine months in the Wisconsin field office before transferring to the New York office, where she was asked to take on a special assignment: the development of an important new intelligence tool.

The FBI is the lead agency for exposing, preventing, and investigating intelligence activities on US soil and protecting critical national secrets and assets. One of the main goals of agents who work in national security is to counter the activities of foreign spies. Through proactive investigations, the FBI work to identify spies and prevent them from learning the nation's most valuable secrets. Special agents who work in the counterintelligence programs need to understand the personalities of their subjects—the spies. Before they attempt to recruit informants, it is important to know the targeted individual's personality traits. When the FBI assigned Rosanne to the New York office in 1981, it did not have an assessment tool that helped agents identify and understand the personality characteristics of their targets; and when the special agent in charge of national security learned that the new female agent in the office had been a practicing psychologist, he sought her out to develop a personality assessment tool.

The personality assessment program that Rosanne developed became a valuable tool agents used to observe and interpret external and internal behaviors of spies. It helped them identify individuals who would become critical informants in the counterintelligence program. Eventually she helped develop assessments for other FBI programs—organized crime, counterterrorism, and white-collar crimes.

In 1981, while Rosanne was developing the personality assessment, she spent time at the FBI Academy in Quantico, where she met the Behavioral Science Unit's criminal profilers, consisting of senior male agents. In addition to developing profiles of unsolved violent crimes to help identify offenders for police agencies, they were conducting a study of serial killers. Although not a new concept, the FBI established this new profiling program to study and formalize the process in assisting other law enforcement agencies.

When the FBI announced it would be soliciting the 56 field offices from across the country to select a criminal profiler coordinator, who would provide the unit with violent crime cases for their program, Rosanne—along with 20 other agents in the New York field office—applied for the position. And despite resistance from the veteran male applicants, the head of the New York office chose Rosanne for the job.

It was at the two-week training for criminal profiler coordinators at the FBI Academy that Rosanne acquired a very valuable skill. She became desensitized to crime scene and autopsy photographs—in other words, says Rosanne, "I didn't need to turn away but instead was able to view them as part of a puzzle."

In the spring of 1984 one of the lead profiling agents from the academy's Behavioral Science Unit contacted Rosanne to ask if she would be willing to transfer to the unit permanently. By the end of the year Rosanne had made the transfer—becoming the FBI's first female profiler.

Who? How? Why? As investigators of violent crimes search for answers, they analyze "almost endless" factors that provide clues to help answer those three questions. And often they turn to profilers like Rosanne Russo to help identify the offender or offenders.

As a profiler, Rosanne developed and provided assessments of offenders. They served as tools for law enforcement agencies to assist in identifying the offender through "psychological traces" left at the crime scene.

There were critical elements that went into the development of a profile. Rosanne used a combination of procedures to develop hers: in-depth interviews of case detectives; objective and comprehensive analysis of crime scene photos, videos, or sketches; reviews of autopsy results; assessment of the victim's personality; and review of similar cases in the area.

"Generally, profilers operated under the premise that there is a great deal of psychological evidence left at the crime scene by the offender," Rosanne says.

Rosanne worked in the Behavioral Science Unit at the academy for less than three years. It was the type of position for which she had prepared for most of her career. And she had been successful in putting dangerous violent criminals behind bars. Yet her time at the academy in the Behavioral Science Unit was dampened by the atmosphere of intimidation and uneasiness. As one of only three female agents working at the FBI Academy in 1984, she felt as if her performance, actions, and behaviors were "constantly under evaluation by the all-male managers."

"My inability to effectively cope with intimidation impacted my focus and work output, causing me to feel less productive and uncomfortable at the FBI Academy," Rosanne says. She requested a transfer to the Washington, DC, field office, where she once again worked in the national security program. "That was one of the hardest decisions I ever made," she says. But Rosanne thrived in Washington, where she was promoted to FBI headquarters and eventually advanced to Cleveland. She was promoted again to an executive-level position and moved to Philadelphia, where she was on September 11, 2001.

In her position as assistant special agent in charge, she served as head of the command post the FBI established to receive telephone calls regarding leads related to the 9/11 terrorist activities. Hundreds of leads had to be followed up, and Rosanne and her multiagency teams worked seven days a week into October.

Despite confronting sexism and intimidation at various levels and locations during her three decades with the FBI, Rosanne retired as a senior-level executive at FBI headquarters in 2008 believing that the majority of colleagues and managers offered opportunities based on her expertise and experiences. She was able to overcome the few who couldn't see past her gender. She had succeeded at her first career as a school psychologist and transferred the skills she had honed there to a career as a profiler in one of the most prestigious law enforcement agencies in the world.

A fictional character in the form of Nancy Drew, girl detective, had influenced a young Rosanne Russo and helped her to

develop a "sense of wonder, self-confidence, and feeling I can do almost anything" and to become a very real-life FBI profiler, who happened to be a woman.

Rosanne Russo.
Courtesy of Rosanne Russo

LEARN MORE

"Behavioral Analysts," Federal Bureau of Investigation
www.fbi.gov/news/podcasts/inside/bau-profilers.mp3/view

"Criminal Profiling: The Reality Behind the Myth" by Lea Winerman, American Psychological Association
www.apa.org/monitor/julaug04/criminal.aspx

ETHEL AND MARLO McGUIRE

FBI Mother-Daughter Special Agents

WHEN MARLO MCGUIRE was in eighth grade, her school invited a speaker from the Federal Bureau of Investigation (FBI) to talk to students about life as an agent in one of the most famous law enforcement agencies in the world. Marlo was intrigued by what she heard, and so were her classmates.

Marlo thought it was a good time to share a little information about her family. She raised her hand and said her mom worked for the FBI. The other kids were impressed when the speaker said he knew Marlo's mom. It began to click in Marlo's mind: her mother was more than a "mom"—she was a woman with a fascinating job! And Marlo's classmates thought so too.

"I was the coolest kid in school for at least a week," Marlo recalled.

Marlo's mother, Ethel McGuire, had joined the FBI after teaching in an inner-city school district and a stint in management for a major chain store. Both were challenging and rewarding; but when she heard the FBI was starting a program to diversify the agency in more ways than one, she was interested. It was 1985, and there were few African American, Latino, or Asian FBI agents. While previously the bureau had been mainly interested in hiring individuals who had accounting, legal, and language backgrounds, it was time for change within the agency. And Ethel McGuire was ready for change in her life too.

Ethel applied in 1985 and entered a list of about 5,000 other hopefuls. A year later she received a call, and she started at the FBI Academy in Quantico, Virginia, in June 1987.

"There were attorneys and doctors and me—a teacher from Tennessee. I was *so* impressed," Ethel says about her classmates at the academy.

She says she wasn't prepared for what she would face at the esteemed training center: "There were a lot of super-duper smart people there." But she adds that extremely high standards were expected of *everyone*.

The training was more militaristic than she had anticipated. She was married with two kids and had grown up in Los Angeles. Living in a dormitory surrounded by a wilderness area with woods and wildlife required a huge adjustment on her part. The physical rigor was a definite challenge too. The recruits had to run at 5 AM and 6 PM every day, but Ethel made herself do additional training by running before and after. "I had to give 300 percent just to keep up," Ethel says. "Even my best was being challenged."

The firearms portion of the training was especially foreign to Ethel. She "didn't understand" shooting. She had never seen a handgun or bullets. It was unnerving when the instructors "screamed and hollered" at the recruits as they practiced shooting. She was too intimidated to ask for help. But she knew the

FBI was merely trying to prepare the students mentally and physically to be in "the real world."

While all the new recruits were held to high standards, Ethel knew that as a woman—and as an African American—she had to make an extra effort. She felt challenged all the way during her training. While many of the males at the academy supported the women recruits, there were "a whole heck of a lot" who didn't, she says.

As only the 47th female African American agent in the history of the FBI, Ethel knew she had an added responsibility. "I had a real purpose for being here—I represented my race and women," Ethel says. "I had to prove we are worthy."

However, it became very clear to Ethel that although her fellow recruits came from various backgrounds and experiences—and that males and females were treated differently in some cases—they all shared a common goal: "the desire to serve." And by the time they had completed the rigorous training, they were ready to serve in the real world of crime.

Ethel's career as an FBI agent began in a position where she conducted background investigations of potential federal judges, prosecutors, and other Department of Justice personnel. Next she moved on to investigating white-collar crimes—theft, fraud, and embezzlement—and then to organized crime, and spent a year as a recruiter in San Francisco. By 1997 she was a drug supervisor assigned to the Criminal Investigative Division of FBI headquarters. Within a few years she was promoted and became a violent crime supervisor with oversight of bank robberies, fugitives, gangs, and drugs. Ethel had experienced a wide and varied career as an FBI agent, and then the terrorist attacks of September 11, 2001, changed everything—including the FBI.

It's been said the world as we know it changed forever after the terrorist attacks on 9/11. The world of law enforcement

EARLY FEMALE FBI AGENTS

The FBI refused to allow women as special agents from 1929 to 1972. However, there were at least four women who entered the ranks earlier, between 1911 and 1928.

Emma R. Hotchkiss Jentzer started as an interviewer of immigrants at Ellis Island and eventually became "a special employee of the Bureau of Investigation of the Department of Justice" (later known as the Federal Bureau of Investigation). She was involved in the capture of a German spy operating in the United States during World War I.

Alaska P. Davidson served as a special agent between 1922 and 1924. Described as a "very refined" woman, she was 54 years old at the time of her appointment and earned seven dollars per day plus four dollars per day when she traveled for agency business. She took her training in New York and afterward was assigned to the Washington, DC, office, where she was involved in an investigation of a fellow agent who was selling confidential justice department information to criminal elements.

Alaska P. Davidson.
FBI.gov

Jessie B. Duckstein started as a stenographer in 1921 and in 1923 was promoted to special agent. She worked in the enforcement of the White Slave Traffic Act, a law that sought to end forced prostitution.

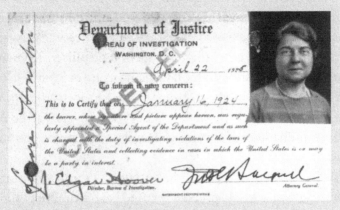

Lenore Houston credentials.
FBI.gov

Lenore Houston served as a special agent from 1924 until 1928. She was single and had completed three years of college. She also was assigned to cases in violation of the White Slave Traffic Act.

Alaska and Jessie were asked to resign when J. Edgar Hoover became director of the bureau in 1924, and the head of the Washington field office where they worked said the office had "no particular work for a woman agent."

Lenore was hired early in Hoover's career, but he asked her to resign after only four years as an agent.

certainly did. National security became a major focus for the FBI. And that focus filtered down to the field offices scattered across the 50 states. Counterintelligence and national security inspections became a major part of the job for agents and supervisors.

Ethel became assistant special agent in charge of two counterterrorism branches within the FBI field office in Los Angeles, where she managed two joint terrorism task forces that together were comprised of more than 200 agents and officers from more than 39 federal, state, and local law enforcement agencies. They were responsible for overseeing all area seaports and airports and investigating all threats to US persons in the Pacific Rim, including Thailand, Australia, Indonesia, Philippines, and South Korea.

As part of her job duties, Ethel attended a special training for supervisors that would prepare them to become more proficient in the world of counterterrorism. She attended ongoing counterterrorism training at the US Military Academy at West Point, New York, where military officers who had served in Afghanistan and other hot spots around the world provided insights into the "real life of terrorism."

The specialized training helped executive managers like Ethel to examine general criminal activities, determining if they supported terrorist activities that threatened national security—and if they did, to mesh the two investigations. The training helped them answer questions like "Why are we doing this?" and helped the field office agents realize that they were supporting a higher calling, such as the military overseas, some of whom were dying "so we can live here free."

In addition, Ethel attended the Naval Postgraduate School in Monterey, California. Here she honed her leadership skills. She heard directly from generals and admirals in the military—

who said, "We need you." Ethel and the other students received instruction about the role the FBI played in national security. That role was very targeted yet "broad enough to prevent another 9/11."

"We all had to be specific with our duties—the military, Central Intelligence Agency (CIA), and the FBI," Ethel explains. "But collectively we played a role."

Ethel continued to move up the ladder within the FBI. By 2008—through an extremely competitive selection process to obtain the senior executive service rank—she was selected as a section executive assigned as chief of the Strategic Information and Operations Center (SIOC) at FBI headquarters in Washington, DC, with oversight of developing major cases and crisis responses for the entire FBI and headquarters divisions.

SIOC was one of several control and command centers during two major events while Ethel was executive—the summer Olympics in 2008 and the presidential inauguration in 2009. Ethel's job duties included managing the FBI's operations center in the United States as it related to the 2008 Beijing (China) Summer Olympics. She coordinated with other law enforcement entities in the United States and China in collecting and disseminating leads and threats that came from around the 50 states, analyzing them and notifying the FBI director, justice department, and the White House when necessary.

During the activities surrounding the 2009 inauguration of President Barack Obama, Ethel headed up the regional command post—covering Maryland, Virginia, and Washington, DC. Again the FBI was on the lookout for "anything not normal." Hundreds of agents monitored command posts around the region and fed information to the central command post.

By the time Ethel retired in 2010, she looked back on over two decades of dedicated service to one of the top law enforcement agencies in the world. She held several high-level and high-profile positions but mostly enjoyed working criminal cases where she collaborated with other agents to bring down offenders.

She recalls one drug case that she and a partner developed over three-and-a-half years. Ethel and her partner teamed up to work with an informant, initially starting with the identification of two "bad guys." Over time they "put the puzzle together," issuing hundreds of search warrants and arrests for drug users and traffickers. She had coordinated the activities of about 500 officers to take drugs and guns "off the streets."

"It was a massive takedown—a huge, huge case," Ethel recalls. "But it was fun."

Ethel says there are cases that "make an impact on your heart" during a career with the FBI. One day she was revisiting a neighborhood where she had been involved in dismantling a drug gang. An elderly man with a big smile on his face approached her squad car. He was carrying a fish; and as he handed it over to Ethel he said, "I can sit on my front porch now." He was safe to go fishing at his favorite fishing spot in the neighborhood, and he wanted to express his gratitude to Ethel by giving her his catch of the day.

In a 2006 interview Ethel said, "I don't consider myself a trailblazer" (in terms of her gender and race). However, she did turn out to be one for her daughter, who in 2004 became an FBI agent. And in so doing, Ethel and Marlo McGuire became the first mother and daughter to work for the FBI in its history.

Marlo's 8th grade career-day visitor from the FBI had sparked her interest in her mother's career, and by the summer after 11th grade she had made the decision to follow in her mom's footsteps. That summer and the next she worked for the FBI as an intern in a special program open to children of agents.

Her duties included mostly answering the phones, distributing mail, and talking to citizens who had complaints or tips. But Marlo was eager to do more, and sometimes she was given more serious tasks—such as retyping transcripts of interviews and highlighting important sections for agents to notice. And she was always intrigued by the activities she saw around the office—like when several agents dashed out the door to a bank robbery or the like.

Marlo earned a degree in accounting and an MBA (master of business administration) and was hired by the FBI in 2004. Her business classes gave her a solid background for the position she eventually took in the agency, but it was the English courses that proved to be most helpful. From the start she was required to write long, complex documents for the cases she worked on. "Pay attention in English," she advises anyone interested in becoming a FBI agent.

She explains it is a common misconception that agents are individuals with law enforcement backgrounds. "In my class of 52, only 8 had prior law enforcement experience," Marlo says.

Marlo was assigned to work fraud, bankruptcy, and public corruption cases. Her cases often involved public officials who abused their powers for personal gain. In one of her first cases in California, she helped bring extortion charges against a businessman who tried to trade special favors with a city official for money. The business owner had connections with elected officials within city government, and he told another businessman, the owner of a car dealership who wanted to acquire old city vehicles for resale, that he would steer the business his way—for a fee (a bribe). The car dealer went to the FBI and told the agency about the illegal arrangement the businessman was proposing. The car dealer agreed to wear an FBI wire and caught the shady businessman on tape offering money for the special favors. A city councilman was also involved in steering the deal to the car dealer. Unfortunately, Marlo's case fell apart when the key witness—the car dealer—died of cancer before going to court.

Marlo says public corruption cases often involve investigations of police officers and other law enforcement personnel, and they are especially "tough to work." Agents are forced to ask "really hard questions" that cause witnesses to "push back."

In a case in Northern California, Marlo had to investigate a police officer who was commander of a drug task force. One of the other officers on the force had given the FBI information that indicated the commander and other officers were stealing evidence—methamphetamine—and selling it for personal gain.

"Police investigations can be unfriendly," Marlo said. "Coworkers want to tell the truth, but they fear they might incriminate themselves or individuals they work side-by-side with."

Interviewing is a significant part of Marlo's job. Her "ability to get people to talk" is a key tool to getting to the "root of a crime." She often has to remind the people she's interviewing that "it's a federal crime to lie to a federal officer."

"It's just relating with people," Marlo says about her skills as an interviewer.

It's especially challenging to interview children who are victims of abuse, she says. It requires spending a great deal of time building a rapport with the children and being careful not to use questions that will lead the kids to give answers they think the agent wants.

But Marlo loves interviewing subjects. It's not uncommon for questioning sessions to last five to six hours. And afterward Marlo has to write up a report describing what she learned—sometimes resulting in a document 25 pages long, or more.

Another part of Marlo's job involves preparing for arrests by doing wiretaps. "People think you can tap a phone at the drop of a hat," she says. "That's not true."

It can take weeks or even months to compile enough information to convince a judge to issue a warrant for a tap. She has to assemble an affidavit that explains to the judge all the evidence she has attempted to collect—unsuccessfully—thereby justifying a tap. Sometimes the document reaches 70 pages or more. This requires her to "learn lawyerly writing," and she often works with an attorney on the documents as she prepares them.

Some days Marlo "hits the streets" to investigate or follow leads. And leads may come from a variety of sources. She might read a story by an investigative reporter in the newspaper and decide to visit individuals mentioned in the article to ask a few questions. Oftentimes Marlo uses the element of surprise to her advantage—knocking on a door to question someone who isn't expecting a visit from the FBI. She can tell a lot from the person's reaction. Are they friendly or unfriendly? An unwillingness to talk may indicate they have something to hide.

Marlo says being African American and a female sometimes works to her advantage. She says at times when she goes into a situation where there is racial tension and feelings of unrest and mistrust, the sight of an African American agent can have an immediate impact by portraying a sense of comfort and trust to citizens.

She recalls a situation in which her gender played a unique role in an apprehension. It was a tense and dangerous standoff where the special weapons and tactics (SWAT) team had entered a neighborhood with a considerable arsenal of resources, including guns and tanks. When the subject of the encounter saw Marlo, he was so shocked at the sight of a woman, he quickly raised his hands in the air and said in disbelief, "Oh my God. It's a girl!" He was a violent, dangerous criminal, but as he sat in the backseat of the squad car, he was "sweet as pie," giving Marlo the names of his accomplices.

In another instance, Marlo was making an arrest in a corruption case in which employees of the Department of Motor Vehicles were selling drivers' licenses to undocumented immigrants in California. The house of one of the suspects had been under surveillance for several weeks, and a plan was in place for making an arrest. Early one morning before daylight Marlo and an all-male SWAT team "breached" the door of the house. As the agents turned their flashlights inside, they found a woman sitting in the room without a stitch of clothing on! All the male agents instinctively turned their backs on the woman. Marlo proceeded to cuff the suspect and find some clothes for her. Both Marlo and the men involved shared many laughs over the reaction!

Ethel and Marlo McGuire.
FBI.gov

Although Ethel and Marlo never worked together on cases (that would be against FBI policy), Ethel greatly influenced Marlo's career. For Marlo, having a mother who was an agent made her path easier. "It's huge. It's always been huge," Marlo says. "My mom is the first person I would call for advice."

"And oftentimes she doesn't like what she hears," Ethel adds.

However, Marlo never doubted the value of having her mother as a fellow agent. She knew she could always rely on an honest answer and sensible counsel. Even other agents looked to Ethel as a caring and devoted supervisor—someone who could be counted on for wise and practical guidance.

When Marlo was transferred to the Los Angeles division, where her mother had worked as a supervisor before her retirement, agents recalled Ethel fondly.

"She's still sort of a legend around here," Marlo says with pride.

LEARN MORE

FBI History
www.fbi.gov/about-us/history

FBI Careers: The Ultimate Guide to Landing a Job as One of America's Finest, 2nd ed., by Thomas Ackerman (Jist Works, 2005)

PART VI

·············

MAJORITY RULES

═══════════════

Police Scientists

"THE WOMAN HAS BEEN missing for a month. Police find her car but no evidence of foul play . . . only a fingerprint and a set of keys. There's a code on one of the keys, which they hope will unlock not only a door but also the mystery of her disappearance."

So goes the plot of an episode in the popular television series the *Forensic Files*, featuring forensic experts who use high-tech science to unravel the most baffling of crimes.

It's only fiction, but actual forensic scientists perform this type of work every day. They are only one type of scientist who uses his or her expertise to help capture criminals. While the idea of bringing these sometimes gruesome stories into homes across America may be a popular fad, the idea of utilizing science to solve mysteries is not new—and most likely won't go out of style. Police work has used science for decades. (In fact, there is evidence of using fingerprinting patterns for identification purposes in prehistoric times.)

Observation and analysis, knowing the structure of a human skull, and recognizing patterns are all scientific competencies that law enforcement personnel use in their day-to-day experiences. Oftentimes proficiency in a science is coupled with other capabilities—as in the case of forensic anthropologists, engineers, and artists. (Forensic artist Lois Gibson reminds readers of her autobiography that "forensic art is about law enforcement, not art.")

While scientific thinking has long been part of police work, the degree and depth has developed over the years. And acceptance of new ideas has not always been easy as police questioned the value of science in police work. As recent as the 1920s and '30s—before Frances Glessner Lee built her miniature crime scenes—investigators unknowingly contaminated and destroyed evidence.

Notably, although both law enforcement and science professions are generally overwhelmingly populated with men, the field of forensic science is dominated by women. One estimate puts the number of female students enrolled in forensic science programs nationally at 78 percent. The lab where forensic identification specialist Cristina Pino works is a seven-person team using science to solve crimes. And the group is 100 percent female! Experts can't identify a clear-cut reason for women dominating the field, but one theory is that young women are inspired by popular television and book series that feature women in forensic labs. The overall emphasis on encouraging girls to explore STEM (science, technology, engineering, and math) careers has had an impact, perhaps. Some experts say women tend to be better at detail work and in team environments. Women working in the field cite their desire to help people and the stability that's lacking in other scientific careers.

FRANCES GLESSNER LEE

....

Turning Crime Scenes into a Science

BRIGHT RED FOOTPRINTS dancing across an otherwise pristine carpet.

The decomposing body of a young woman.

A dead man sprawled facedown on the floor—clad in blood-saturated pajamas

This horrific scene was the creation of a Chicago socialite whose life experiences led her down a surprising and bizarre career path—one that allowed her to interlace a childhood fascination with an adult passion and that would forever change the way detectives investigate crime scenes.

Frances Glessner's doting mother described her as a "delightful, clever and precocious little girl." Her resourcefulness and intelligence would serve her well as an adult crime fighter, but when she was born, to a wealthy farm machinery manufacturing executive and his wife, no one could have imagined Fanny's remarkable future.

Born into a luxurious and lavish lifestyle, Fanny was nine years old in 1887 when her family moved into the exclusive Prairie Avenue neighborhood of Chicago. Mr. Glessner had hired a renowned architect to design a house that would declare his status in Chicago society and at the same time give his family a "cozy" residence. "Monumental and fortress-like" were words used to describe the pink granite mansion that became known as Glessner House.

Little Frances—Fanny—grew up there with her parents and older brother, George. (During the summers the Glessners stayed at their other residence—a thousand-acre estate called the Rocks—in New Hampshire.) Frances drank from crystal glassware and ate her meals on gold-monogramed china at a table that sat 18 people under the gold-leaf ceiling of the dining

Glessner House, 1800 South Prairie Avenue, Chicago, Illinois.
Library of Congress HABS ILL,16-CHIG,17-2

Fanny Glessner, 1890.
Glessner House Museum, Chicago, IL

room at Glessner House. She and George were schooled by a private tutor in the mansion's schoolroom—designed so the noisy children could slip in and out without disturbing the rest of the household. A spiral staircase led from the schoolroom to the two children's bedrooms, which were separated by a secret passage leading from one to the other.

When Frances was a young lady, she followed the rules set down by society for a woman of her class. She spent a year touring Europe and then returned to debut in Chicago society. By the time she was 20 years old, in 1898, she had married an attorney named Blewett Lee, and by 1906 she had three children. The marriage was not a good one. In 1914, after a five-year separation, Fanny sued for divorce, charging Mr. Lee with desertion. It came as "no surprise to their friends," according to a Chicago newspaper.

Fanny had fulfilled all the expectations society required of her over the years. She had married, bore children, and abandoned her dream of pursuing a career in the medical field. (Her father always said, "A lady doesn't go to school!") Now she was ready to shake things up a little; she was about to embark on an adventure that would change her life and the future of crime investigation forever.

THE DEATH INVESTIGATION SYSTEM

Some officials think we need to reevaluate and overhaul our inconsistent system for investigating unexpected or suspicious deaths nationwide. It's a system that has roots in the British royal monarchy, where kings used individuals known as "crowners" to investigate deaths of subjects—in order to collect death taxes. (The word *crowner* evolved into *coroner* in the American colonies.)

Today there is no uniform system in place throughout the 50 states. Some states use coroners, others use medical examiners, and others use a combination. It's the duty of a death investigator to examine the scene, review the victim's medical records, perform autopsies, and determine the manner and cause of death. The results are crucial to insurance and estate settlements and murder investigations.

Medical examiners are usually doctors with years of training and experience, but not all are board-certified forensic pathologists, which means they do not have specialized training to learn what to look for when performing autopsies and conducting other death investigation essentials. Coroners might be medical doctors, but in some states the only prerequisite is that an individual be of legal age (18 or 21) and a resident of the state. Coroners are frequently elected to their positions—they may be sheriffs or funeral home directors.

A botched death investigation can result in innocent people going to prison, guilty people going free, and murder victims being categorized as accidental deaths. In 2009 the National Academy of Science recommended a uniform system in which every state would hire only board-certified forensic pathologists as medical examiners. It advocated moving away from a coroner system.

In the 1920s Fanny began to spend time with Dr. George Burgess Magrath, an old college friend of her brother and the medical examiner for the City of Boston. His job duties required him to determine the cause of death of victims of accidents and crimes. He had earned a reputation for solving some of the city's most baffling cases. Dr. Magrath used scientific methods of observation and analysis to investigate crime scenes. But, he told Fanny, his task was made extremely difficult by the detectives who arrived at the scene before him. He complained they often unknowingly tampered with evidence—walking through bloody footprints, sticking their fingers into bullet holes in the victim's clothing, or moving dead bodies. The detectives and other law enforcement officials at the time were unaware of the role science should play in crime investigation.

Fanny was intrigued with her friend's work. At first she confined herself to listening and talking to Dr. Magrath about his theories, but soon she was not content to participate in this emerging field from the sidelines. She began to study and research the field of forensics—or medico-legal studies, as it was called.

By the 1930s Fanny had become the sole recipient of her family's vast fortune. Her mother and brother had died, and when her father died she inherited all of his estate. She spent most of her time at the Rocks in New Hampshire. She felt so strongly about the work Dr. Magrath was doing that in 1932 she donated $250,000 to Harvard University to establish a department that would focus solely on medico-legal studies. She also donated about 1,000 legal medicine books to establish a library at the university. "For many years I have hoped that I might do something in my lifetime that should be of significant value to the community," Fanny said at the opening of the new library.

The Department of Legal Medicine was the first forensic pathology program of study in the United States. Dr. Magrath became a professor in the program, where students were trained to become medical examiners and to use his groundbreaking methods.

To ensure that medical examiners could do their jobs well, it was important that detectives and other law enforcement officials understood forensics also. It not only increased the chances of maintaining an uncontaminated crime scene—it also gave the police new methods and tools to conduct their investigations of violent crimes. Dr. Magrath and the staff from the Department of Legal Medicine began to offer the Harvard Seminars in Homicide Investigation. These short, weeklong events were taught twice a year and were open to police detectives and other homicide investigators across the country.

When the homicide detectives arrived eager to begin their intensive crime investigation class, they were perplexed to see a "queenly looking woman with her high, white coiffure and tiny gold-rimmed eyeglasses," and what looked like dollhouses set up in the seminar room. More than one must have thought he had mistakenly signed up for the wrong class! But they would soon learn how Fanny and her dolls would help them become first-rate investigators.

Miniature making had been an "appropriate" hobby for little girls and even young women in the late 1800s and early 1900s.

Designing and decorating the little rooms, sewing clothes for the petite figures, and painting tiny portraits to hang on the walls offered females opportunities to demonstrate their creative aptitudes. It was an approved pastime for Fanny, and she rather enjoyed it. She became especially accomplished at the tasks that required an acute attention to detail. Her parents hoped it would distract her from her very "inappropriate" affinity to medicine and science.

But as her mother had noted early in Fanny's childhood, she always was a clever and highly intelligent individual; and those characteristics stayed with her into adulthood. While miniature making continued to absorb Fanny as a middle-aged woman, she had also spent years developing her other obsessions—medicine, science, and crime investigation—through her association with Dr. Magrath and the Department of Legal Medicine at Harvard. Now Fanny had found a unique way to transform her very divergent passions into a meaningful endeavor to help teach rookie and veteran detectives about the science of investigation and forensic science.

At first glance the mystified detectives who entered the seminar rooms assumed the miniature dioramas held doll families living an idyllic existence in their elaborately constructed houses—miniscule mousetraps unobtrusively situated in a corner, tiny ironing boards scorched with realistic burn marks, door keys that worked in intricate locks, calendars turned to the correct month and year, half-peeled potatoes by the kitchen sink, and lights that went on and off. But nothing about the dioramas was intended for children. They all depicted bloody, gruesome scenes of often violent deaths.

An accident or a gruesome murder? Or was it a murder-suicide? How did the perpetrator enter the room? Did he or she leave behind any clues? Did the dead couple know the attacker? Was there a struggle? What does it all mean? What can be learned by analyzing the details of the scene? Those were the kinds of questions the detectives at the Harvard Seminars in Homicide Investigation would grapple with. And thanks to Fanny's eerie creations, they learned to find answers through a realistic and practical method of police work combined with science and medicine.

Fanny used the facts surrounding actual police files to develop her dioramas. She accompanied police to crimes scenes, visited morgues, and observed autopsies—all the while gleaning details to include in her diminutive tableaus. Sometimes she fused several actual cases into one diorama, and she substituted made-up names—"Homer Cregg, Wilby Jenks, and Sergeant Moriarty"—for the real ones.

Along with the meticulously fashioned rooms, she provided cards containing additional information to help students solve the mysteries. To ensure longevity, the actual solutions to the crimes were never revealed, maintaining the mysteries of the dioramas. Year after year a new batch of students used the uncanny dioramas to help them become astute forensics experts. The methods they refined and the new skills they perfected were as critical as the actual solutions of the crimes.

Fanny hired a full-time carpenter named Ralph Moser to build the basic structure of the rooms, using a scale of one inch to one foot. Then Fanny went to work on the details, often using a magnifying glass as an aid. She knit socks for victims using straight pins as knitting needles, smeared lipstick stains on pillowcases, and embedded bullets in walls. It took about three months at a cost of $1,000 to complete each. (It took Fanny three days to make the burn on the ironing board look convincing.) She gave each of the 20 scenes a name: Three-Room Dwelling,

Parsonage Parlor, Dark Bathroom, Burned Cabin, Pink Bathroom, Kitchen, and Unpapered Bedroom.

To help students fully appreciated the macabre death rooms, Fanny advised, "The inspector may best examine them by imagining himself a trifle less than six inches tall." In the "Pink Bathroom" the students witnessed a dark-haired woman with a wound around her neck sprawled on the floor, a pair of tiny crocheted flip-flop slippers on the fringed throw rug, a miniscule roll of toilet tissue hanging haphazardly on the holder, and fluffy pink towels draped over towel racks. Was she strangled? Or was it suicide?

A man dead in his bed was the centerpiece of the "Burned Cabin" diorama—complete with charred boards as walls of the log-constructed "Hy-Da-Way." He was one of two men who lived in the cabin—an uncle and his nephew. The dead man was the uncle, and the nephew had run from the cabin as it burned. In the statement the nephew made to police, he insisted he had been asleep also but had managed to escape the burning

"Parsonage Parlor" doll.
Corinne Botz

structure. The fact that he was fully clothed made police suspicious of his story.

And there was the especially gruesome "Parsonage Parlor," where a teen victim lay with a knife protruding from her partially decomposed chest. Dark pools of blood stained the floor near her head. Pieces of mail stacked up by the door indicated the homeowner had been gone for some time.

During the seminars police detectives worked in pairs—each with a different diorama. Over two to three days the pair studied their model—observing, theorizing, analyzing—trying to determine what had taken place at the pint-sized scene. At the end of the seminar each team explained how they would go about solving the crime and offered a "reasonable explanation" of their reasoning in solving the crime. The instructor of the seminar questioned the detectives and challenged their findings—oftentimes pointing out "some obscure, overlooked detail."

Some of the scenarios were designed to teach police some simple, easily observable medical principles. An example of one that Fanny incorporated into an *apparent* suicide scene was the concept of "lividity"—a discoloration of the skin at the location of blood settling in an area of the body at the time of death. Blood will always settle in the area of the corpse that is closest to the ground at the time of death. For example, if a person dies while lying on his back, gravity draws the blood to that area and lividity sets in. In Fanny's cleverly designed scenario, several clues led observers to determine the victim—lying facedown—had died from a suicide. However, the obvious lividity in the *lower back* was a sure sign to the most knowledgeable observers that someone had turned the corpse over *after* death had occurred.

Fanny called her series of grisly crime scene dioramas "Nutshell Studies of Unexplained Death." She adapted an old police

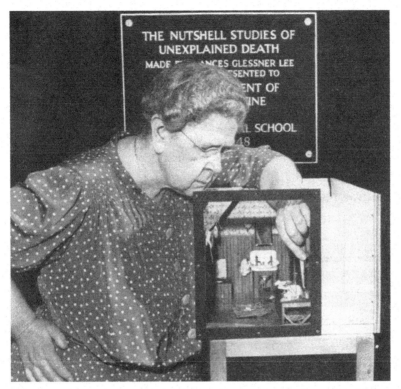

Frances Glessner Lee with one of her nutshell dioramas, 1949.
Courtesy of Glessner House Museum, Chicago, Illinois

adage that seemed to sum up her ideas about crime investigation: "Convict the guilty, clear the innocent, and find the truth in a nutshell." (A nutshell being "something of small size, amount, or scope.")

The Nutshell Studies of Unexplained Death became valuable tools to students of forensics for years. Harvard University continued to utilize Fanny's creations throughout the 1940s and '50s. In 1966—four years after Fanny's death—they were sent to the Maryland Medical Examiner's Office in Baltimore, where they continue to captivate visitors and students.

"People take them as seriously as any other crime scene," Dr. David R. Fowler, the chief medical examiner for Maryland, said in 2004. And although modern-day students rely on much more sophisticated tools to hone their craft, Dr. Fowler claimed, "I have never seen any computer-generated programs that even come close."

Frances Glessner Lee refused to let tradition and conventional thinking prevent her from doing what she truly desired in life. She found a way to transform a seemingly frivolous pastime into a valuable career that shaped the history of law enforcement and crime investigation.

LEARN MORE

Glessner House Museum
www.glessnerhouse.org

The Nutshell Studies of Unexplained Death by Corinne Botz
(Monacelli, 2004)

LOIS GIBSON

·················

Empowering Victims of Violent Crime

"WHEN THE LIFE IS being choked out of you and you feel you only have seconds to live, all you have left in the world are your thoughts."

And that's what Lois Gibson had—only her thoughts. She thought of her little brother, the fact that she hadn't had children yet, that she hadn't lived as much as she wanted to. She wasn't ready to die, but she believed that was her fate.

Lois was 21 years old in 1972, living alone in a cozy apartment in Los Angeles. She had grown up in a loving home in Kansas but had moved to California to make her way in the world. One night she opened her door to a man whom she shouldn't have trusted. And it changed her life forever. The stranger put a choke hold on Lois's throat so tight that she passed in and out of consciousness as the man brutally assaulted her.

After the violent encounter there were a few very specific physical characteristics that Lois vividly recalled. Her attacker's complexion was "pasty white." He had a "bluish five o'clock shadow" around his goatee. He had "dark eyebrows."

The near-death experience stayed with Lois for a long time. And while it made a very dark imprint on her life for years, she managed to turn it into a positive. It was because of the assault that Lois was compelled to combine her love of art and her desire for justice into a career as a forensic artist.

Lois had always had a strong artistic side, and after the attack moved to Texas to pursue an art degree. As a student at the University of Texas in Arlington, she worked at a popular amusement park as a portrait artist. Next she moved to Austin, where she finished her art degree, and then on to San Antonio. There Lois began studying to become a maxilla-facial prosthesis technician at the University of Texas Health Science Center, making artificial facial features for people after surgery or accidents. Surprisingly, the skills and science principles she picked up there served her well in the career she would eventually embrace.

The River Walk in San Antonio—a popular tourist attraction meandering throughout the downtown along the San

Antonio River—became a favorite spot for Lois to relax and enjoy the shops and restaurants that lined the sidewalks. She approached shop owners and asked if she could set herself up with an easel and paint portraits of tourists

Lois Gibson, forensic artist.
Courtesy of Lois Gibson

on weekends. Soon she was making enough money to become a sidewalk artist full time. She put aside her aspiration to become a prosthesis technician and committed to a career as an artist.

Despite her growing success, Lois seemed in search of something. By 1978 she had made another move—to Houston, where she continued to be haunted by the memory of her attack in Los Angeles. One night as she was watching television she was again reminded of the terrifying experience. There was a news story about a rapist who had attacked a woman. As the police described the attacker, who had gotten away, Lois became incensed. The description was as generic as it could be—brown hair, brown eyes, medium height. That could be almost any male in Texas! And Lois knew from experience that the victim probably could provide much more precise detail and that a capable portrait artist could produce a rendition of the man just from the verbal description. She knew it with all her heart—as a victim and as an artist.

A few of Lois's friends helped her prove her point. She asked them to give verbal descriptions of individuals they saw in stores and other public places. As they talked, she drew. Always her friends were astounded by the close resemblance between the actual person and the sketch Lois produced. She seemed to possess a skill that certainly could be of value to the police—and give peace of mind to victims. Now all she had to do was convince law enforcement officials.

"Hi, my name is Lois Gibson and I'm an artist who can do drawings of suspects from witness descriptions." Over and over she made her pitch on the phone and in person. But the Houston Police Department wasn't interested. They didn't need an artist. Until one day in June 1982 her call was transferred to a Lt. Don McWilliams, who listened and invited Lois to show him what she was talking about.

"Come on down, girl!" he said.

Finally Lois's persistence had paid off. She proved her point by asking a department secretary to go to a cell and come back ready to describe one of the suspects held there. In front of the officer and a crowd that had gathered, Lois deftly drew the face of the criminal who the secretary had seen. Everyone was astounded at the likeness. They were ready to consider that this woman had a unique ability that could be of use to the police department.

"No matter how hard I worked or how many successes I had, I was still an outsider," Lois said. In 1985 she had worked for three years as an on-call sketch artist for the Houston Police Department. She had been very successful in helping solve numerous cases—one in every three that she worked on. But she was called on only sporadically. It had been an uphill battle to gain acceptance with the officers.

The idea of an artist contributing to police work was new to most departments in the country, and, Lt. McWilliams aside, Houston was especially resistant. Many of the officers couldn't see the benefit of Lois's skills. Some refused to ask for her help because she was a woman in a man's world. Others saw her as an outsider. Many couldn't take her seriously because she was a civilian—not trained in law enforcement. When she learned about the FBI Academy's forensic artist school, she knew that was the place for her to gain respectability.

Late in 1986 Lois was accepted to the two-week forensic artist course at the FBI Academy near Washington, DC. "This was a chance to be myself, surrounded by people who understood completely," Lois said.

Lois and the other students in the highly specialized class received instruction from experts in the field. Anthropologists taught skull reconstruction, a photographer illustrated photo retouching with an airbrush, and a forensic artist showed age

progression techniques. Students learned to complete a full
frontal face drawing based on input from victims who had seen
only the profile or parts of a suspect's face. Lois was introduced
to a valuable tool called the *FBI Facial Identification Catalogue*—
almost 200 examples of each facial feature. The catalogue was
especially helpful when working with children who struggled
with words to describe features or people whose first language is
not English. With the catalogue they could point to the specific
characteristic as they grappled to develop an image of suspects.

The FBI course was a tonic for Lois. She bonded with other
forensic artists who shared her passion, and she was equipped
with new skills and tools of her trade. Returning to Houston,
Lois was ready to get to work.

"Tonight my drill team is going to perform during half-time
at the homecoming football game. It's my first time to perform,"
a young girl explained to Lois.

The 15-year-old sophomore was in a hurry to complete her
session with Lois, who was constructing a drawing of a man
who had abducted and sexually assaulted her.

The girl's comment and eagerness to talk about the drill-team
performance inspired Lois. It showed that the victim was refus-
ing to let the attack consume her life. It was a healthy sign that
the girl would eventually get beyond the terrible experience.

As Lois drew, the girl talked. She described facial features
and chose a chin and lips from samples. Finally the sketch was
completed, and Lois turned her paper for the girl to see. She
gasped—the sketch looked just like her attacker. Now it was up
to the police to find him.

Lois's sketch was distributed among the various law enforcement agencies—including the county sheriff's office where the
case originated and the Houston Police Department—and to the
public. A detective in the homicide division of the police depart-

FBI FORENSIC FACIAL IMAGING TRAINING

Forensic artists need to have a wide variety of skills—not only in the art field. They need to be able to read signs that a person they are interviewing is telling the truth. They must be ready to appear in a courtroom and testify under pressure. And a forensic artist must be sensitive to interviewing traumatized victims. The FBI offers training in the highly specialized area of forensic art to select individuals.

The FBI forensic facial imaging training is now a three-week course for members of law enforcement agencies, government crime labs, and the military. FBI forensic artists and other noted law enforcement and academic professionals teach the course through lectures, demonstrations, and role-playing.

The course involves learning facial anatomy, drawing different racial groups, drawing accurately and quickly, and studying facial aging techniques. Students learn how to be excellent listeners, how to pose questions that improve a victim's memory, how to interview children, and how to work with the media.

Students must apply for entry into the program. Although it's not a prerequisite that applicants are trained artists, the class includes intensive drawing. In order to be considered for the program, applicants must be actively working in the forensic art field or be designated by a law enforcement department, a crime lab, or the military to produce artist composites. The program also accepts international students who meet the same requirements.

ment spotted Lois's sketch and recognized it as a man he had arrested for the murder of his mother-in-law. He was currently out of jail, having posted bond. When the detectives showed the 15-year-old victim a mug shot of the man, she immediately identified him as her assailant. In addition, a person had seen the sketch and reported it on the Crime Stoppers hotline. Within a very short time the man was apprehended and charged with aggravated sexual assault of the girl.

Sometimes Lois was called upon to help identify victims in the morgue. It was a difficult facet of her job; but she looked at it as a way to find justice for a victim, bring closure to a family, or help a "restless soul find peace." Lois's years of experience and her expertise helped her reconstruct faces that had been destroyed by elements in nature or by humans.

Sometimes Lois's work was less unsettling in nature. "I need help finding my two brothers. They just vanished from my life," pleaded a young woman in her thirties who had last seen her brothers when they were one and two years old. She was four when she was separated from them after the death of their mother. Providing pictures of the boys when they were young, she asked if Lois could do an age progression of the two. Maybe then she could find her long-lost siblings.

It was a first for Lois, but after meeting the woman and seeing the pictures and video of the two little boys, she was up for the challenge. She knew certain facts about aging of facial features due to her training at the FBI Academy. For example, the shape of nostril holes and eyebrows remain the same from infancy to adulthood. But some features do change—irises occupy less of the eye openings and the nose lengthens. Hair darkens and cowlicks don't go away.

Using all she knew about aging and facial features, Lois produced two pictures of the boys, who would now be men. She

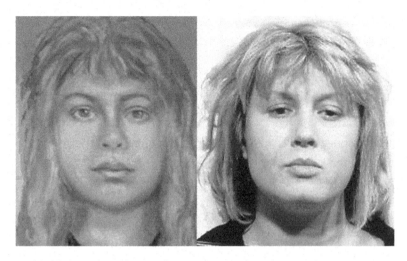

A sketch by Lois Gibson of a crime suspect who was later apprehended.
Lois Gibson, Forensic Art Essentials, 2007

also had a crucial resource in her toolbox—she knew some-one who worked on the television show *Unsolved Mysteries*. She called him and convinced the show's producers to air the story of this unsolved mystery.

Before the episode ended, the woman had been put in touch with her brothers! It was one of Lois's extraordinary cases put to rest with a happy ending.

People often asked Lois how she mustered the will to do her difficult work. While she admitted there were dark days, she believed the ultimate end product of her labors gave her inspiration to continue. She helped stop violent criminals from doing more harm, but most important, she helped secure justice for innocent victims.

"I've worked with the victims . . . and together we've taken something unseen—their tortured memories—and created evidence." Then it's up to dedicated law enforcement officials to take the evidence and track down the criminals. "When they do, then I have empowered those victims."

LEARN MORE

FBI's Forensic Facial Imaging Training
www2.fbi.gov/hq/lab/html/ipgu3.htm

Northwestern University Center for Public Safety
http://sps.northwestern.edu/program-areas/public-safety

CRISTINA PINO

············

"First of All, I Had to Learn English"

CREATING CHIC DESIGNS for the fashion houses of Europe or analyzing human body decomposition—it was a tough career choice for Cristina Pino when she was a young girl growing up in Naples, Italy.

She wanted to "travel all over the globe and be exposed to a myriad of cultures," so the world of fashion beckoned. But she also was captivated by the science world of forensics after reading *Death's Acre: Inside the Legendary Forensic Lab the Body Farm—Where the Dead Do Tell Tales* by Dr. William M. Bass. Cristina was transfixed by the work of the author and his students at the Anthropology Research Facility (also known as the Body Farm) in Tennessee, where they studied the decomposition of human bodies in various environmental conditions. A career in forensic science ultimately won out—partly because Cristina wanted "to make a difference."

Long before Cristina made her career choice, she was growing up in Naples, where her loving parents, Aldo and Ornella, instilled in her and her younger sister, Emilia, a sense of empathy and generosity as they shared meals around the family's big dinner table. Cristina took her parents' advice to heart when she was only a small child. She had left for school one day wearing a new pair of shoes but returned home at the end of the day with an old and worn pair. When questioned by her mystified mother, Cristina admitted she had given her shoes to another little girl in her class who was very poor.

Cristina's appreciation of art and culture were gifts from her grandfather, Armando. Every Sunday Cristina, Emilia, and their grandfather explored the museums, churches, and markets of Naples. The National Museum of Capodimonte, containing artworks from the early 1700s; Teatro di San Carlo, an opera house established in 1737; Napoli Sotterranea, the labyrinth of cavities and tunnels that snake under the city of Naples; Galleria Umberto, a glass-domed gallery of businesses, shops, and residences built in the late 1800s; and the ruins of Pompeii—they were Cristina's playgrounds.

By the time Cristina was ready to enter college in 1998, she knew with all her heart she wanted to work in the forensic field. However, she could not find an appropriate course of study for forensic anthropology in her native Italy. So she first earned a bachelor's degree in sociology and then a master's degree in criminology.

Cristina knew that it would be nearly impossible to do her life's work in Italy. Individuals who work in a forensic lab in Italy must have a degree in a "hard science"—such as biology, physiology, or chemistry—and they must be part of a police force. She could eventually become a private consultant; however, that would require a great deal of experience and time to establish herself.

She remembered her mother's words of encouragement: "You are a brave and intelligent woman, and if you believe and study hard, you can accomplish anything you want." And this gave Cristina the courage to pursue her goal to work in forensic science—despite any obstacles. For Cristina, it would mean leaving the people she loved to go to a foreign country where she must first learn a new language and culture.

In 2006 Cristina moved by herself to West Lafayette, Indiana, where she took a job teaching Italian at Purdue University while continuing to improve her English skills. By then she had met and married the love of her life, Armando Poeta, in Italy. Because he was in the Italian air force, he was not free to move with Cristina to the United States, but he fully supported her dream to work in the forensic field. "He helped me become what I am today," Cristina says of Armando. "He always was telling me that one day I would succeed."

Cristina's English improved daily. "At the beginning it was very hard," she recalls. "I could not express myself the way I

wanted. It was very frustrating when people did not understand me—my emotions and personality." But she was driven by her desire to someday pursue her career in forensics.

Cristina Pino and her husband, Armando Poeta.
Courtesy of Cristina Pino

After two years, before beginning any forensic studies, Cristina decided to return to Italy to be with her husband. She decided to put her dream "on hold." In 2008 she joined Armando, who was stationed in Sardinia. After about a year Armando saw that Cristina was not happy and regretted her decision to leave the United States and put her studies aside. He encouraged her to return to the States and continue. Armando remained in Italy with the Italian air force.

"Cristina e-mailed regarding the Forensic Science Academy. She said that she was in Italy but would be back in the United States soon," Dr. Janis Cavanaugh, coordinator of the academy in Industry, California, explains.

Cristina had been searching for a forensic school that would provide the skills and experience she knew she would need in order to work in the forensic field in the United States. She found just what she was looking for at the academy.

"It was during my time at the forensic academy that I got a better understanding of the forensic career. It was exciting and intimidating at the same time," Cristina remembers. "But after the first day my fear disappeared."

Almost immediately Dr. Cavanaugh saw Cristina as a special student—a hard worker and someone driven by her goals to overcome all barriers to work in her chosen profession. "Cristina is a unique individual. She is a shining star," Dr. Cavanaugh says of her former student.

The 18-week Forensic Science Academy offered classes in fingerprint identification, photography, crime scene and death investigation, DNA and biotechnology, ballistics, map reading, and report writing. Students learned how to roll a proper set of fingerprints and palm prints, collect and preserve evidence, identify various types of gangs, identify types of wounds, analyze blood spatter patterns, and re-create a crime scene, among other skills. Experts from a variety of fields helped instruct—a DNA researcher, judge, coroner, homicide detective, polygraph examiner, and anthropologist.

Cristina also completed two internships—with the Los Angeles County Department of Coroner and the Beverly Hills Forensic Unit. She started her first only five months after arriving in Los Angeles from Italy. "I was nervous, disoriented, and very clumsy," Cristina recalls about the coroner's internship experience. "Despite these feelings, I had a terrific time there," she adds. "I was exposed to so many deaths. Some of them were violent, like a car accident or shooting. Some others were natural, with decomposed or mummified bodies."

She was assigned to help a forensic attendant—a "right-hand man" of the death investigator. She learned to process a body in terms of taking photographs of the deceased and to collect and document evidence like hair and nails.

"A unique experience it was when I had the chance to observe an autopsy," Cristina remarks. "It is not a mystery how an autopsy is performed. You can go online to find a video. But being there is completely different," she says.

"I observed with trepidation how the medical examiner was performing an exterior and interior analysis of the body. Any tattoos, scars, and wounds were documented and measured. Each organ was analyzed and documented with care. I will never forget that day and the smell," Cristina says.

Cristina's internship with the Beverly Hills Forensic Unit was equally compelling: "It was with them that my desire of working in the forensic field increased. It was ideal for me because I really could perceive and understand what a crime scene investigation job looked like."

"I strongly believe that an internship is a main key in order to pursue this career. It gives the opportunity of getting a real taste of what you will be doing daily and what to expect from this career," Cristina advises.

While Cristina was attending the academy, she worked as a server at a restaurant. Armando had taken a leave from the Italian air force for two years to join her in America, and in 2012 he left the military to join his wife permanently.

In 2013, after years of dreaming, sacrificing, and working diligently, Cristina landed a job as a forensic identification specialist (FIS) with the Torrance (California) Police Department Forensic Identification Specialist Unit. Today she works with a team of six—all women: a supervisor (who, like Cristina, is a new immigrant—from England), a senior forensic identification specialist who specializes in latent print examination, and three forensic identification specialists who work mostly out in the field. Cristina's area of expertise is crime scene investigation. She is responsible for the complete documentation of crime scenes and the identification, processing, and collection of physical evidence.

"Without any doubts, the best part of my job is its uniqueness. Each crime scene is different, because it tells an unrepeatable story," Cristina remarks.

She says she has had to develop better critical thinking skills as a result of her profession: "It changed the way I see and look for things. When I process a crime scene I try to go behind the simple observation, outside the box."

She recalls a quote from a book by Arthur Conan Doyle (*A Scandal in Bohemia*): "You see, but you do not observe."

"Working in this field, I understand the meaning of this quote. An item of evidence found at a crime scene is telling us something important. So don't just overlook it, but pause and think. That item of evidence is just a piece of a puzzle that must be assembled in order to understand what happened," Cristina says. "I think this is the beauty and the best part of my job."

INVESTIGATING A CRIME SCENE

Footprints, dried saliva stains, blood droplets—all valuable evidence that tell a story at a crime scene. When a serious crime is committed, it is essential to collect and preserve evidence at the scene. The process is a painstaking adventure that helps solve a mystery. The steps are precise and carefully pre-scribed in order to avoid contaminating evidence.

The first official on the scene is a first responder, who quickly sees to the needs of victims or anyone who was injured. An officer establishes a pathway through which any of the investigators will enter and exit. The officer uses barricades or tape to secure the scene, keeping unwanted individuals from enter-ing the area.

Investigators begin to document the scene and the evidence. They use a variety of tools: note-taking, photography, sketching, and/or videography. Law enforcement personnel use a specified pattern as a guide to search: spiral, grid, strip, quadrant, or wheel.

It takes a skilled and experienced investigator to distinguish between what is critical evidence and what is not. Every single object found at the scene cannot be considered evidence to analyze.

At a hit-and-run scene, blood and tissue, fabric, hair, and fibers might be collected as evidence; at a burglary there may be broken glass, shoeprints, or tool marks; and at a homicide investigators might collect weapons, bullets, fingerprints, blood, or soil.

Some objects are obviously evidence; others are less obvious. Trace evidence includes very small—even microscopic—objects such as blood, tissue, fibers, or fingernail scrapings. These are collected in

Typical Crime Scene Search Patterns

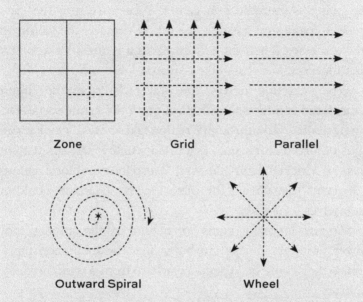

Zone   Grid   Parallel

Outward Spiral   Wheel

a variety of ways—tweezers, hand swabs, or vacuums, for example.

After identifying evidence, investigators must meticulously package it. The packaging is critical. Some is as simple as a paper envelope for evidence such as paint chips, glass shards, or soil. Blood can be tricky though. Wet blood placed in an airtight container can grow moldy, making it lose its value as evidence. It should be collected on a swab, allowed to dry, and placed in a paper envelope. After they gather all the appropriate evidence at the crime scene, the investigators submit it to a crime lab for analysis.

Investigating a crime scene can be a lengthy and expensive process. But it is a critical step in solving crime.

Cristina deals with a wide variety of crime scenes in her day-to-day work. She regularly investigates residential burglaries. A typical situation would begin with a dispatch to an officer from the police communication center. After assessing the crime scene to make sure it is safe, the officer contacts the victim and any witnesses. Then the officer places a request for a forensic identification specialist—like Cristina.

When Cristina arrives, the officer describes the circumstances and conducts a walk-through of the crime scene. During this initial walk-through Cristina takes notes. "I look for any signs of forced entry, such as a pried window screen, shattered glass, or a kicked door," she says. "I also look for blood, because it happens that during the intrusion the assailants could cut themselves," she adds.

She also looks for items left behind by the suspect: tools, gloves, flashlight, or cigarette butts. She is aware of shoe impressions—they could be located anywhere from a windowsill to a bathtub.

Next Cristina conducts a technical investigation, taking interior and exterior photos of the scene. In the exterior photos she focuses on the point of entry made by the burglar. Any damages on doors, windows, or screens are photographed. "I usually use a ruler and take close-up photos in order to show an accurate representation of the size of the damage," she says.

Interior pictures center on the damage left behind when a burglar ransacks drawers and closets. Some scenes are more complicated than others and require Cristina to take additional steps like taking measurements and drawing a sketch. Cristina takes photos of clothing, jewelry boxes, documents, or any personal items tossed on the floor. Sometimes items are moved from one place to another by the suspect. "This is a crucial aspect," Cristina notes, "because from that specific object I can collect a

Cristina and a coworker examine evidence at a crime scene.
Photographer Mark Boster, Copyright © 2014 Los Angeles Times. Reprinted with permission

sample of touch DNA." (Touch DNA is a forensic method that analyzes skin cells left behind when assailants touch victims, weapons, or something else left at the crime scene.) An example would be a flashlight recovered on a patio when the victim is certain he or she always kept the item in the drawer of a bedside table.

"When I find prints, I feel very satisfied!" Cristina says.

After conducting her investigation at the crime scene, Cristina heads to the office, where she books the evidence in the property room and then writes her report. She uses a $1.5 million laboratory, which was built with money seized from drug dealers, to help analyze some of the evidence.

One of Cristina's main duties is to testify in court as an expert witness. As a new forensic identification specialist, she worried about her first appearance in a courtroom situation. "I had to remind myself to not move my hands while I was talking, because it could be distracting. Being Italian, it is very hard to not gesticulate," she jokes.

Cristina practiced for days as she prepared for her first court appearance. "My main concern, as a foreigner, was my strong accent. Was I understandable? How would the judge, clerks, and lawyers perceive me? A million times I asked myself those questions," she recalls. "For days I reviewed my case in front of a mirror, listening to my voice tone, to how I was expressing myself."

"After my testimony I felt relieved," Cristina says. "I was impressed how easy it was and how I could share my knowledge without letting my accent interfere with my testimony!"

Cristina admits that there are unique challenges to her profession. "Some scenes can affect your mind and your emotions. It is very important that a forensic specialist detaches him or herself from the feelings that a crime scene and a victim can raise. Believe me, it is not easy!" she confesses.

Another obstacle can be the long hours and working weekends and holidays at crime scenes. "When you choose this career path you need to be ready to put on hold—and sometimes sacrifice—your private life with your family and friends," Cristina says.

"It could happen that I can get called in the middle of a party or a romantic dinner with my husband, and without hesitation I need to respond, because it is my duty to serve my department and community. I am kind of married to my job."

But she adds, "I always feel excited. My excitement rises even more when we get complex and high-profile crime scenes."

Looking back on her career pathway, Cristina feels proud of the choices she made as she followed her dreams: "This career required a total commitment and a lot of dedication. So many times I felt alone and nostalgic. I missed my family and my husband. But the desire to become a forensic specialist was stronger. So I did not give up. I succeeded!"

LEARN MORE

Criminalistics: Forensic Science, Crime, and Terrorism, 2nd ed., by James E. Girard (Jones & Bartlett Learning, 2011)

East Los Angeles College, Administration of Justice
www.elac.edu

National Museum of Capodimonte (Museo di Capodimonte)
http://cir.campania.beniculturali.it/museodicapodimonte

Occupational Outlook Handbook, Bureau of Labor Statistics
www.bls.gov/ooh

Opportunities in Forensic Science Careers by Blythe Camenson (McGraw-Hill, 2009)

RESOURCES

· · · · · · · · · · · · · · ·

CAREER OPPORTUNITIES IN LAW ENFORCEMENT

Amtrak Police Department
http://police.amtrak.com
The Amtrak Police Department is a national police force committed to protecting the passengers, employees, and stakeholders of the Amtrak railroad corporation. More than 500 sworn and civilian personnel at more than 30 locations in 46 states conduct a range of behind-the-scenes and frontline security measures to ensure Amtrak employee, passenger, and infrastructure safety and security.

Department of Homeland Security (DHS)
www.dhs.gov
Over 240,000 employees in the DHS work to secure the nation from threats. Jobs range from aviation and border security to emergency response, from cybersecurity analysts to chemical facility inspectors, and many others.

Department of Justice (DOJ)
www.justice.gov/careers
Established in 1789, the DOJ enforces the law and defends the interests of the United States, ensures public safety against foreign and domestic threats, provides federal leadership in preventing and controlling crime, seeks just punishment for those guilty of unlawful behavior, and ensures fair and impartial administration of justice for all Americans.

Environmental Protection Agency (EPA)
www2.epa.gov/enforcement
The EPA's mission is to protect human health and the environment. It also enforces regulations and helps companies understand federal environmental requirements. If companies fail to meet the national standard, the EPA can help.

National Park Service (NPS)
www.nps.gov
Since 1916, the NPS has safeguarded more than 400 places and preserved natural and cultural resources of the National Park System for future generations.

Private Detectives and Investigators
www.bls.gov/oes/current/oes339021.htm
These independent investigators gather, analyze, compile, and report information regarding individuals or organizations or detect occurrences of unlawful acts or infractions of rules in private establishments.

Secret Service
www.secretservice.gov
The purpose of the Secret Service is to ensure the security of the president, vice president, their families, the White House, the vice president's residence, national and visiting world leaders, former presidents, and events of national significance. The Secret Service also

protects the integrity of the currency and investigates crimes against the national financial system committed by criminals around the world and in cyberspace.

Transportation Security Administration (TSA)
www.tsa.gov
The TSA protects the nation's transportation systems to ensure freedom of movement for people and commerce.

US Postal Inspection Service
https://postalinspectors.uspis.gov
The federal law enforcement, crime prevention, and security arm of the US Postal Service supports and protects the postal service and fights criminals who attack the nation's postal system and who misuse it to defraud, endanger, or otherwise threaten the American public.

Women in Peacekeeping
www.un.org/en/peacekeeping/issues/women/womeninpk.shtml
As women become increasingly part of the United Nation's peacekeeping force, they are deployed in all areas—police, military, and civilian.

HANDS-ON EXPERIENCES

City of Golden, Colorado, Youth Citizens' Academy
www.cityofgolden.net/city-services/citizens-police-academy
This program is designed to provide teens with an inside look at law enforcement and to increase understanding between young citizens through education and interaction with members of the police department. The academy includes demonstrations in crime scene investigation, K-9 patrol, SWAT (special weapons and tactics), and hands-on police scenarios. Many other cities offer similar youth academies.

Florida Association of Police Explorers
www.youtube.com/watch?v=eFI-FmZio3Q
This state organization helps young people explore a career in law enforcement. Students between 14 and 17 learn policing skills such as being aware of surroundings at a shooting scene, tracing down bullets, working in a parent staging-area at a school shooting, calming parents down, and working at an incident command center. Many cities have similar police explorer programs. Check local departments.

National Young Leaders Conferences
www.envisionexperience.com
These conferences develop leadership skills offered in various career pathways. Middle and high school students gain real-world experience in law enforcement fields, including law, crime scene investigation, national security, intelligence, foreign affairs, and the diplomatic corps.

Youth Leadership Program
www.fbinaa.org/FBINAA/Training/Youth_Leadership_Program.aspx
The Youth Leadership Program is a weeklong training event held every summer for high school students at the FBI Academy. Candidates must be 14, 15, or 16 years old. Interested candidates should possess a desire to gain knowledge in the American system of criminal justice, including police organization, leadership, and the structure and operation of criminal courts.

PLACES TO VISIT IN PERSON OR ONLINE

CIA Museum
https://www.cia.gov/about-cia/cia-museum
This museum supports the Central Intelligence Agency's operational, recruitment, and training missions and helps visitors better understand the CIA and its contributions to national security. The collection includes clothing, equipment, weapons, insignia, and other memorabilia that were designed, manufactured, and used specifically for intelligence operations.

Coast Guard Museum

https://www.uscg.mil/hq/cg092/museum

Located at the US Coast Guard Academy in New London, Connecticut, this museum contains artifacts that span the 225-year history of the US maritime service. Visitors may stroll the grounds of the academy while watching the flag raising, walking the decks of the sailing vessel *Eagle*, and reviewing the Corps of Cadets.

Drug Enforcement Administration
Museum and Visitors Center

www.deamuseum.org

This museum and visitors center educates the American public on the history of the Drug Enforcement Administration and on the impact of drug addiction from past to present. It's located in Arlington, Virginia, and admission is free.

New York City Police Museum

www.nycpm.org

Dedicated to preserving the history of the world's largest police service, this museum is home to the largest publically accessible material collection and archive holding of the New York City Police Department (NYPD) and includes artifacts, documents, photographs, and other ephemera. The collection tells stories of the NYPD as well as New York City's history and its changes in society over a period of 400 years.

Office of the Chief Medical Examiner

900 West Baltimore Street
Baltimore, Maryland 21223
410-333-3250
info@ocmemd.org

Frances Glessner Lee's actual Nutshell displays may be viewed by special appointment at the Office of the Chief Medical Examiner, Baltimore, Maryland.

VIDEOS

Book Discussion on *A Different Shade of Blue*
www.c-span.org/search/?searchtype=All&query=policewomen
In this C-SPAN video, author Adam Eisenberg talks about his book *A Different Shade of Blue: How Women Changed the Face of Police Work.*

Kimberly, Foreign Service Officer, Diplomatic Security Special Agent
http://careers.state.gov/youtube/kimberly_fss
A Foreign Service specialist with the US State Department and former FBI agent talks about characteristics the department looks for in hiring new recruits.

US Women Military Police
www.youtube.com/watch?v=dVy-D9cooiM
This US Army video shows women in military police training with the Seventh Infantry Division in Yakima, Washington.

NOTES

....

INTRODUCTION

"Huh! A good joke": "Policewomen for Lorain," *Rock Island (IL) Argus*, May 25, 1907.

New York's Auburn prison: Shulz, *From Social Worker to Crimefighter: Women in United States Municipal Policing*, 10.

"If the hand of the law": Arthur J. Brinton, "Now We Have with Us the Lady Cop." *Ogden (UT) Standard*, July 17, 1913.

PART I: THE EARLY MATRONS

In 1826 Rachel Welch: Schulz, *From Social Worker to Crimefighter: Women in United States Municipal Policing*, 10.

Anna was a teenager: "Police Stations in Chicago Are Lousy," *Chicago Day Book*, September 21, 1915.

"A matron would invite": "In the Interest of Delicacy," *New York Times*, May 12, 1882.

"outrageous state of things": "Interest of Delicacy."

"an outrage on": "Jail Matrons," *St. Paul (MN) Daily Globe*, October 20, 1887.

SADIE LIKENS (1840–1920)

He was convicted of forgery: Annette L. Student, "Sadie Likens: Patron of the Fallen," *Colorado Heritage*, summer 2001.

She tended sick and dying: Schulz, *From Social Worker to Crimefighter: Women in United States Municipal Policing*, 14.

"a most genial of women": Rider, *The Denver Police Department: An Administrative, Organization and Operational History, 1858–1905*, 320.

"elegant cold lunch": Rider, *The Denver Police Department*, 262.

"American flags," "delicacies": Schulz, *From Social Worker to Crimefighter*, 14.

"two of the most notorious criminals": O'Hare and Dick, *Wicked Denver: Mile-High Misdeeds and Malfeasance*, 151.

"the most celebrated case": O'Hare and Dick, *Wicked Denver*, 150.

"stacked with stolen goods": O'Hare and Dick, *Wicked Denver*, 150.

"the notorious Watson gang": O'Hare and Dick, *Wicked Denver*, 149.

"great and noble work," "nobody could be found": Charles Hartzell, *A Short and Truthful History of Colorado During the Turbulent Reign of Davis the First* (Whitefish, MT: Kessinger, [1894] 2010), 73.

"blue eyes, dark hair": "Chicanery," *Rocky Mountain News*, August 31, 1894.

"I would hardly have mixed": "The Governor Together with Several City Officials of Denver Are Charged by Ex-Police Matron Likens with Having Withheld a Letter Addressed to Her," *Summit County (CO) Journal*, September 1, 1894.

"boiling with indignation" . . . *"did conspire together"*: "Chicanery."

Sidebar

"the smaller ones in the front": "Our History," Woman's Christian Temperance Union, Australia, www.wctu.com.au/pages/history.html.

"oldest voluntary, non-sectarian": "Early History," Woman's Christian Temperance Union, www.wctu.org/history.html.

ALETHA GILBERT (1870–1904)

"immoral places," "suggestive": Linda Espana-Maram, "Creating Masculinity in LA's Little Manila: Working-Class Filipinos and Popular

Culture, 1920s–1950s." *Southern California Quarterly* 90, no. 3 (Fall 2008): 335–38.

"wayward boys and girls": "Her Ears Hear Women's Woes," *LA Times*, October 4, 1914.

"Keeping children out of court" . . . *"defective"*: "Official Mother to Save City's Kids," *Scranton Truth*, September 21, 1914.

"While I talk to many girls": "Her Ears Hear."

Historian and author Janis Appier: Appier, *Policing Women: The Sexual Politics of Law Enforcement and the LAPD*, 74; Price, "'City Mother' Dispenses Love to All in Trouble," *Santa Cruz Evening News*, December 22, 1914.

"lighten their burden of sorrow," "cheerful frame of mind": "Police Matrons Divide Work," *LA Herald*, July 30, 1906.

"If we can teach one woman": "Educating the Women Prisoners," *Salem (OR) Daily Capital Journal*, April 4, 1910.

"About two-thirds [of the women in the jails]": "Educating the Women Prisoners."

"To shut women up": "Low Wages Cause Downfall of Majority of Girls, Says Matron," *Wichita Beacon*, August 26, 1911.

"hostile," "fat, blue-eyed infant": "Return Whiting Baby to Mother," *LA Herald*, September 27, 1910.

"immorality and crime": Appier, *Policing Women*, 104.

"I was constantly meeting": "'City Mother' Dispenses Love."

"kind-faced" . . . *"eyes [that] are kind and blue"*: Dille, "LA 1st City in World to Establish City Mothers," *Altoona (PA) Tribune*, February 2, 1916.

"For all her kindly matronliness": "LA 1st City."

In 1915 the City of Los Angeles: "Pennant Stand Appointments," *Journal of Social Hygiene* 1, American Hygiene Association, 1914–1915.

"masquerading as a man": "Sexless Man Is Arrested," *Wichita Daily Eagle*, September 12, 1915.

"I was born a girl": "Sexless Man."

"When City Mother Gilbert arrested me": "Sexless Man."

"I have wronged no one": "Posed as a Man for 25 years," *Fort Wayne News*, September 2, 1915.

"afflicted with the silver screen bacillus": Miriam Teichner, "LA 'City Mother,' Busy Saving Girls Lured by the Movies," *Ottawa Journal*, November 5, 1920.

He was the son of a single mother: "City Mothers to Assist Genius," *Oakland Tribune*, July 11, 1915.

"soothed and solved" . . . *"grievances"*: "Interesting Westerners," *Sunset: The Magazine of the Pacific and of All the Far West* 46, February 2, 1921.

"While orange groves": Uthai Vincent Wilcox, "A City That Has a Mother," *Rotarian*, April 1929.

PART II: POLICEWOMEN

A Detroit policewoman: Eleonore L. Hutzel, *The Policewoman's Handbook* (New York: Columbia University Press, 1933), 178–179, https://archive.org/stream/policewomanshand00hutz#page/178/mode/2up.

Some of the first who: Kerry Segrave, *Policewomen: A History*, 2nd ed. (Jefferson, NC: McFarland, 2014), 47, 48.

ISABELLA GOODWIN (1865–1943)

"impenetrable mystery": "The Latest Bomb Outrage," *New York Times*, March 19, 1912.

it took the detective skills: "Woman Made Municipal Detective," *Meriden (CT) Morning Record*, March 2, 1912.

"What do you know": "New York's Only Woman."

"Sleepyhead looks good to me": "New York's Only Woman."

"My, I never saw such excitement" . . . *"Those gambling ladies"*: "New York's Only Woman Detective," *Spanish American*, May 25, 1912.

"attractive and gracious" . . . *"middle aged and respectable looking"*: "The First Municipal Woman Detective in the World," *New York Times*, March 3, 1912.

"She told me to turn my back" . . . *"suggestionist"*: "New Thought Cure Cost $2," *New York Times*, May 16, 1913.

"Sister, my dear sister!" "Are you happy?": "Mrs. Goodwin Nabs a Spook," *New York Times*, May 11, 1913.

"pretty little blonde girl," "demonstrator": "Mrs. Goodwin Nabs a Spook."

"overindulgence in cream soda": "A Heilmanotiseur Nabbed," *New York Sun*, August 31, 1911.

"One of New York's best known," "If thou wouldst catch a hubby": "Study Widows' Ways of Catching Husbands, Seeress Tells Detective," *Washington Herald*, June 2, 1912.

"All of them assumed I wanted a husband": "New York's Only Woman."

"Sometimes it's pretty hard": "Woman Detective Relates How She Captures," *New York Sun*, August 11, 1912.

"the subject of jest and cartoon": "Woman Made Detective."

"Well, Eddie the Boob turned": "First Municipal Woman."

"shedding money like a canary": "Woman's Scheming Gets Taxicab Bandits," *Chicago Day Book*, February 27, 1912.

"My flesh creeps sometimes": "First Municipal Woman."

"first municipal woman detective": "First Municipal Woman."

"I do not care for the distinction": "Woman Detective Seeks More Honors," *Daily East Oregonian*, March 9, 1912.

"looking anxiously about": "Mrs. Goodwin and Other Detectives Catch Five at Opera House," *New York Times*, March 28, 1916.

"kept her from any influences": "Witnesses Say They Denied Seeing Patrolmen Shot from Dread Shillitoni," *New York Times*, February 26, 1914.

In another case a crowd: "Arrest a Gypsy Princess," *New York Times*, February 12, 1914.

"I consider it a personal matter": "Woman Detective Kept Wedding Secret," *New York Evening World*, November 28, 1921.

"I threw myself": "First Municipal Woman."

"It's not a career": "Making More Money: Lieutenant Isabella Goodwin," *Philadelphia Evening Public Ledger*, June 10, 1921.

"small figure". . . *"The things I have learned"*: "First Municipal Woman."

GRACE WILSON (1882–1956)

"There is one blanket": "Police Stations in Chicago Are Lousy," *Chicago Day Book*, September 21, 1915.

"colored girl": "Police Stations Lousy."

"full of cigarette stubs": "Police Stations Lousy."

"When we change clothes": "Police Stations Lousy."

"The officers are always looking" . . . *"When I was first put in"*: "Police Stations Lousy."

"My great aim is to insist": "First Negro Policewoman Joined LA Force in 1916," *Ebony Magazine*, September 1954, 32.

During the early 1900s: "The Chicago Race Riot of 1919," History Channel, www.history.com/topics/black-history/chicago-race-riot-of-1919.

"Who are you?": "Policewoman Grace Wilson Shows Mettle," *Chicago Defender*, November 2, 1918.

"I am a police officer": "Policewoman Shows Mettle."

"culture and refinement": "Policewoman Shows Mettle."

"Policewoman Makes Ten Arrests": *Chicago Defender*, April 20, 1918.

"highly complimented": "Policewoman Makes Ten Arrests."

"looked down the lonesome road": "Primitive Man Battle over Love of Woman," *Chicago Defender*, August 31, 1918.

"invaluable aid to young girls": "A Scrap Book for Women in Public Life," *Chicago Defender*, September 7, 1929.

"seen the sights": "Boy Wanderer Is Here to See Fair," *Chicago Defender*, May 6, 1933.

"Scott and I are taking lessons": "Mrs. Wilson Learns to Shoot," *Chicago Defender*, May 4, 1918.

Sidebars

"My great aim is to": "First Colored Lady Officer," *LA Times*, September 24, 1916.

"the female Booker T.": "First Colored Lady."

"I didn't need my eyes": "First Negro Policewoman," 32.

"a striking figure": "Blackfoot Woman Has Unique Job," *LA Times*, December 28, 1924.

"crack shot": "Chief and Mrs. Wades-in-the-Water," *Boston Globe*, March 1, 1925.

MARY SULLIVAN (1884–1950)

"Carter's Pills presents": "The Case of the [Scheming] Bridegroom," *Policewoman*, Old Time Radio, www.oldtimeradiodownloads.com /crime/police-woman/the-case-of-the-steaming-bridegroom -1947-06-29.

"a long green gown": Sullivan, *My Double Life*, 17.

"That's no career for a lady": Sullivan, *My Double Life*, 17.

"badger game" . . . "boyfriend": Sullivan, *My Double Life*, 21.

"It's only when I'm drunk": Sullivan, *My Double Life*, 27.

"proper enough for a party": Sullivan, *My Double Life*, 32.

"behind a mahogany desk": Sullivan, *My Double Life*, 36.

"of the clinging vine species": Sullivan, *My Double Life*, 35.

"*hard as a steel plate*," "*hair bleached*": Sullivan, *My Double Life*, 46.

"*torrid dance halls*" . . . "*negro colony*": Sullivan, *My Double Life*, 54.

"*expensive and nimble-witted lawyers*," "*well-laid traps*": Sullivan, *My Double Life*, 55.

"*gorilla-like*," "*Everybody against the wall!*": Sullivan, *My Double Life*, 62.

There were different versions: Margaret Sanger, *My Fight for Birth Control* (London: Faber & Faber, 1932), 32.

Sidebar

"*Why when a woman does*": "Criminals Have Little Love for This Woman," *Detroit Free Press*, June 3, 1908.

"*among the foremost living*": "Most Famous Woman Sleuth," *Washington Post*, March 17, 1912.

"*It's an infallible means*": "Criminals Have Little Love."

"*It is absolutely impossible*": "Criminals Have Little Love."

PART III: POLICE OFFICERS

"*the pistol-packin' mammas*," "*shooting iron*": "Powder-Puffs 'n' Pistols," *Washington Post*, October 2, 1943.

Sidebar

Little Word, Big Impact: Clay Risen, *The Bill of the Century: The Epic Battle for the Civil Rights Act* (New York: Bloomsbury, 2014).

MOIRA SMITH (1963–2001)

"*If my mom was back*": Patricia Smith, e-mail to author, January 16, 2015.

"*Life can be annoying*": P. Smith, e-mail.

"*freak out*": Kathleen Conaghan, interview by author, February 9, 2015.

It was when Kathleen: Conaghan, interview.

"*She took my Yankee hat*": Phil Hirschkorn, "9/11 Victims Share Heartache with Moussaoui Jury," CNN, April 6, 2006, www.cnn.com/2006/LAW/04/06/moussaoui.victims/index.html.

"*As we waited with thousands*": Jim Smith, e-mail to author, January 15, 2015.

"who was always on top": Irish Tribute, February 20, 2002, www
.irishtribute.com/tributes/view.adp@d=236920&t=1648242
.html.

"A crush of sheared metal". . . *"A tangled metal mass"*: Finder, "The
Subway Crash," *New York Times*, August 29, 1991, www
.nytimes.com/1991/08/29/nyregion/subway-crash-irt-driver
-charged-5-deaths-crash-shuts-line-ties-up-city.html.

"the worst New York subway disaster": Finder, "Subway Crash."

For a time Moira worked: J. Smith, e-mail.

"in control of the situation," "Don't look!": Martin Glynn, www.moira
smith.com.

"No words are appropriate": Edward Nicholls, interview by author, February 14, 2005.

"Until every person was out": Conaghan, interview.

"gave Moira a big hug": Conaghan, interview.

"I would take one minute": Conaghan, interview.

Sidebar

"create a meaningful tribute": Cliff Kuang, "The Near-Impossible Challenge of Designing the 9/11 Museum," *Wired*, May 14, 2014, www
.wired.com/2014/05/911-museum-3/.

JULIA GRIMES

"My dad agreed": Julia Grimes, e-mail to author, December 19, 2014.

"I spent every dime," "All I wanted": Grimes, e-mail, December 19, 2014.

"I read it and became infatuated": Grimes, e-mail, December 19, 2014.

"My strategy was": Grimes, e-mail, December 19, 2014.

"Surrounded by too much": Grimes, e-mail, December 19, 2014.

"We need pilots": Grimes, e-mail, December 19, 2014.

"most unexpected change of course," "the most remarkable experience":
"About Julia," True North Focus, www.truenorthfocus.com
/About_Julia.html.

"doing pushups and running": "About Julia."

"aerobic death," "stressful challenge": Grimes, e-mail, December 19,
2014.

"Some very good acting": Grimes, e-mail to author, April 6, 2015.

"Undercover work is so different": Grimes, e-mail, April 6, 2015.

"Many emotions occurred simultaneously": Grimes, e-mail, April 6, 2015.

"grow operations": Grimes, e-mail to author, February 17, 2015.

"Those are potato plants!", *"And sure enough"*: Grimes, e-mail, February 17, 2015.

"I picked up many a dead body": Grimes, e-mail, February 17, 2015.

"who think they have gotten": "Juneau Assistant District Attorney Richard Svobodny Tapped to Become Alaska's First Cold Case Prosecutor," State of Alaska Department of Law, November 1, 2005, www.law.state.ak.us/press/releases/2005/110105-Svobodny.html.

"I'm very proud," "wherever they are": "International Marijuana Trafficking Ring Indicted," US Drug Enforcement Administration, April 24, 2006, www.dea.gov/pubs/states/newsrel/seattle042406 .html.

"an adventure," "opportunity to do things": Brant Tataboline, "Trooper Director Proud of Her Troops," *Anchorage Daily News*, February 1, 2004, quoted in Wells and Alt, *Police Women: Life with the Badge*, 26.

Sidebar

"He is credited with the detection": Grimes, e-mail, February 17, 2015.

"It didn't even faze him": Grimes, e-mail, February 17, 2015.

"If they didn't pick it up": Grimes, e-mail, February 17, 2015.

"Truth be told": Grimes, e-mail, February 17, 2015.

"It was probably the most unique delivery": Grimes, e-mail, February 17, 2015.

PART IV: POLICE CHIEFS

"old bachelors" . . . *"practically silenced all opposition"*: "She Is a Police Commissioner," *Boston Daily Globe*, June 10, 1894.

"small of stature," "believes that comfort should be paramount": "She Is a Police Commissioner."

Only about 13 percent . . . *Changes have occurred*: Peter Horne, "Policewomen: Their First Century and the New Era," *Police Chief* 73, no. 9 (September 2006), www.policechiefmagazine.org/magazine /index.cfm?fuseaction=display_arch&article_id=1000&issue _id=92006.

RHODA MILLIKEN (1895–1992)

"dolled up like a Christmas Tree," "enough rouge": "Raid by Police-women," *Washington Post*, March 3, 1919.

"Kid, if you go": "Raid by Policewomen."

Rhoda Milliken had been one: Frances Fuchs, "Barnard Alumna Heads Lady Police Force in Washington," *Barnard Bulletin*, February 21, 1949.

"personality" . . . *They would be paid $1,460*: "45 Classic Beauties Needed on Cop Force; Doll Babies Barred," *Washington Times*, May 19, 1921.

"willful girls," "recreational parlor": "Woman Cop at Union Station Watches for Fair Flirters," *Washington Herald*, May 4, 1919.

"well-known fact that boys and girls": Lily Rowe, "Appropriation for Women Police Squad Under Fire," *New York Tribune*, September 7, 1919.

"the instrument of the devil" . . . *"lure of the movies"*: "Fears War as Morals Get Looser," *Washington Times*, July 4, 1921.

"indecent dancing" . . . *"undesirable and dangerous acquaintances"*: "Fears War."

"follow-up workers" . . . *cost an estimated $400 per person*: "Fears War."

The cost per person in 2010: "The Cost of a Nation of Incarceration," *Sunday Morning*. April 23, 2012, www.cbsnews.com/news/the-cost-of-a-nation-of-incarceration/.

"We find that there is usually something": Howard Wentworth, "New Bureau to Trace Happy, Unhappy Casuals of Life Here," *Washington Post*, May 11, 1936.

"This system would greatly aid": "Emotional Girls Warned Not to Go to Washington," *Tipton (VA) Tribune*, June 10, 1942.

"It is a complicated and discouraging problem": "Emotional Girls."

"If your daughter is emotionally unstable": "Emotional Girls."

"Parents who have not bothered": "Emotional Girls."

"It seems funny," "all the bobby sox girls": Martha Kearney, "Army, Navy Officials Blamed for Urging Girls to Come to Capital," *Tipton (VA) Tribune*, October 21, 1944.

"tread the straight and narrow": Ragsdale, "Capital's Juvenile Delinquents Give No. 1 Policewomen Headaches," *Pampa (TX) Daily News*, July 27, 1942.

"smiling, crinkly-eyed wisp": Ragsdale, "Capital's Juvenile Delinquents."

"nervous strain of war," "It's an emotional release": "War Makes Heroes out of Some People but Others Turn Out to Be Shoplifters," *Rio Grande Valley (TX) Morning Star,* January 16, 1944.

"as an accepted part" . . . *"great network"*: Milliken, "The Role of the Police Women's Bureau in Combating Prostitution," *Federal Probation* 9, no. 2 (1943): 20.

"biggest headache": "They Start with Crime as Children," *Atlanta Constitution,* April 6, 1950.

She said there was nothing new . . . *"Maybe we will spend more"*: "They Start with Crime."

"holding the line," "about 3,600 per year": Davis, "Washington, by Citywide Effort, Cuts Down Juvenile Delinquency," *Atlanta Constitution,* July 15, 1945.

"The best thing": Davis, "Washington Cuts Delinquency."

"all the things that embarrass": "They Start with Crime."

"with a sparkle in her eye," "In this job you have to smile": Mary Hornaday, "Capital Not So Bad as Painted," *Christian Science Monitor,* May 22, 1942.

Sidebar

"It's that tom-tommy" . . . *"Any music played on a saxophone"* "Music: Indecent," *Time,* August 10, 1925.

"hit two of our senses at once" . . . *"Reform astronomy too"*: "Reform's Vast Empire," *Washington Post,* September 22, 1925.

PENNY HARRINGTON

"Fat, homely, double-chin," "A freak like you": Harrington, *Triumph of Spirit: An Autobiography by Penny Harrington,* 70.

"Over my dead body": Harrington, *Triumph,* 51.

"What do you mean": Harrington, *Triumph,* 52.

"Don't you come complaining": Harrington, *Triumph,* 68.

"lousy": Jennings Parrott, "No Cop-Outs for Woman Chief," *LA Times,* January 24, 1986.

"Don't choke 'em; smoke 'em": "Portland's Tarnished Penny," *Time,* April 14, 1986.

"Ban the hold, stop the killing": Harrington, *Triumph,* 206.

In a Survey: Wallace Turner, "Police Chief in Rift with Her Officers," *New York Times*, January 31, 1986.

"I cannot have those men": Harrington, *Triumph*, 209.

"Under Fire, Woman Quits": Wallace Turner, *New York Times*, June 3, 1986.

"First Woman to Head Big-City Police": Bob Baum, Associated Press, June 2, 1986, www.apnewsarchive.com/1986/First-Woman-to -Head-Big-City-Police-Department-Resigns/id-72c223fa7ed 66ccb9d5acac393fa2b8b.

"tarnished penny": "Portland's Tarnished Penny."

"a ride on a bucking bronco": Harrington, *Triumph*, 222.

JODY KASPER

"I was an ok student": Newberry, "Meet the Chief: Northampton's Capt. Jody Kasper Credits Guidance Counselor for Her Career," *Mass Live*, June 25, 2015, www.masslive.com/news /index.ssf/2015/06/meet_the_chief_northamptons_jo.html.

"My mom and sister": Jody Kasper, interview by author, August 20, 2015.

"giant structures like Ferris wheels": Kasper, e-mail to author, August 12, 2015.

She became a member of an elite group: Kasper, e-mail, August 12, 2015.

"Pick out what's interesting": Newberry, "Meet the Chief."

"walking a beat": Snow, *Policewomen Who Made History: Breaking Through the Ranks*, 48.

"lot of activity in the dark": Kasper, interview.

"gave chase": Kasper, e-mail to author, August 24, 2015.

"Detectives get a lot of interesting cases": Kasper, interview.

"I certainly have noticed differences": Snow, *Policewomen*, 55.

"It was good police work": Kasper, e-mail, August 24, 2015.

"usually with people under the influence": Kasper, interview.

"He was punching people": Kasper, interview.

"Every once in a while": Hugh Zeitlin, "Northampton Car Dealership Dealing with Stolen Airbags," *CBS News*, September 17, 2014, www.cbs46.com/story/26558939/northampton-car-dealership -dealing-with-stolen-airbags.

"felt that it took too long": Evan Bleier, "Massachusetts Man Facing Charges After Alleged Gumball Machine Attack at Pizze-

ria," UPI, July 14, 2014, www.upi.com/Odd_News/2014/07/14/Massachusetts-man-facing-charges-after-alleged-gumball-machine-attack-at-pizzeria/7531405350700/.

"I, Jody D. Kasper": "Swearing in of Northampton Chief of Police Jody Kasper," YouTube video, July 1, 2015, www.youtube.com/watch?v=peUnCupTWQU.

"I've never paid much attention": "Swearing In."

Judy's colleague: Kasper, e-mail to author, September 18, 2015.

"The SRO isn't just there": "School Resource Officer Returning to Northampton High School After Two-Year Vacancy," US News Hub, July 31, 2015, massachusetts.newshub.us/news/item/07-31-2015/School%20resource%20officer%20returning%20to%20Northampton%20High%20School%20after%20two-year%20vacancy.

"expanded strategies," "enhance public safety": "Swearing In."

"I am incredibly fortunate": Snow, *Policewomen*, 151.

"I've always been a huge believer": Newberry, "Meet the Chief."

"I believe that as women": Snow, *Policewomen*, 55.

"impassable": Kasper, interview.

"do more," "do better": Kasper, interview.

"I don't want to brush over": "Swearing In."

"We have missed our children's bedtimes": "Swearing In."

"I admire Jody": Kasper, e-mail, August 24, 2015.

"It's really neat": Kasper, e-mail, August 24, 2015.

PART V: FEDERAL AGENTS

"the only woman employed": "Woman Sleuth Seeks Facts," *LA Times*, September 27, 1907.

However, one female customs: "Smuggling Not Easy," *Washington Post*, March 4, 1900.

In 1969 President Richard Nixon: Wells and Alt, *Police Women: Life with the Badge*, 14.

ROSANNE RUSSO

"I had an overpowering feeling": Rosanne Russo, e-mail to author, December 5, 2014.

"I didn't need to turn away": Russo, e-mail, December 5, 2014.

"almost endless": Russo, e-mail, December 5, 2014.

"psychological traces": Russo, e-mail, December 5, 2014.

"Generally, profilers operated": Russo, e-mail, December 5, 2014.

"constantly under evaluation": Russo, e-mail to author, March 5, 2015.

"My inability to effectively cope," "That was one of the hardest decisions": Russo, e-mail, March 5, 2015.

"sense of wonder": Russo, e-mail, December 5, 2014.

ETHEL AND MARLO MCGUIRE

"I was the coolest kid": Dan Carrison, *From the Bureau to the Boardroom: 30 Management Lessons from the FBI* (New York: AMACOM, 2009), 232.

"There were attorneys and doctors": Ethel McGuire, interview by author, February 21, 2015.

"There were a lot of super-duper": E. McGuire, interview, February 21, 2015.

"I had to give 300". . . "the real world": E. McGuire, interview, February 21, 2015.

"I had a real purpose": E. McGuire, interview, February 21, 2015.

"the desire to serve": E. McGuire, interview, February 21, 2015.

"real life of terrorism": E. McGuire, interview, February 21, 2015.

"so we can live here": E. McGuire, interview, February 21, 2015.

"We need you," "broad enough to prevent another 9/11": E. McGuire, interview, February 21, 2015.

"We all had to be specific": E. McGuire, interview, February 21, 2015.

"anything not normal": E. McGuire, interview, February 21, 2015.

"bad guys" . . . "off the streets": E. McGuire, interview, February 21, 2015.

"It was a massive takedown": E. McGuire, interview, February 21, 2015.

"make an impact on your heart," "I can sit on my front porch": E. McGuire, interview, February 21, 2015.

"I don't consider myself a trailblazer": "Mother-Daughter Duo on Life Inside the FBI," NPR, November 24, 2006, www.npr.org /templates/story/story.php?storyId=6533673.

"Pay attention in English": Marlo McGuire, interview by author, March 12, 2015.

"In my class of 52": M. McGuire, interview, March 12, 2015.

"tough to work" . . . *"push back"*: M. McGuire, interview, March 12, 2015.

"Police investigations can be unfriendly": M. McGuire, interview, March 12, 2015.

"ability to get people to talk" . . . *"It's just relating with people"*: M. McGuire, interview, March 12, 2015.

"People think you can tap a phone": M. McGuire, interview, March 12, 2015.

"learn lawyerly writing": M. McGuire, interview, March 12, 2015.

"hits the streets": M. McGuire, interview, March 12, 2015.

"Oh my God," *"sweet as pie"*: M. McGuire, interview, March 12, 2015.

"breached": M. McGuire, interview, March 12, 2015.

"It's huge": M. McGuire, interview, March 12, 2015.

"And oftentimes she doesn't like": E. McGuire, interview by author, April 23, 2015.

"She's still sort of a legend": M. McGuire, interview by author, April 23, 2015.

Sidebar

"a special employee": The Federal Reporter, vol. 259, October–November 1919, 1920 (St. Paul, MN: St. Paul West, 1920), 683; "Grand Jury Indicts Two for Treason," *New York Times*, December 7, 1918.

She was involved: *Federal Reporter*, 683.

"very refined": "McLean's Agent Bares Theft of Means' Diaries," *Oakland Tribune*, May 21, 1924.

"no particular work for a woman": Athan G. Theoharis, ed., "Alaska P. Davidson," *The FBI: A Comprehensive Reference Guide* (Phoenix: Oryx, 1999), 322.

PART VI: POLICE SCIENTISTS

"The woman has been missing": "Skeleton Key," *Forensic Files*, www .forensicfiles.com/skeleton-key.html.

"forensic art is about law enforcement": Gibson and Mills, *Faces of Evil: Kidnappers, Murderers, Rapists and the Forensic Artist Who Puts Them Behind Bars*, 256.

One estimate puts the number: Kate Mather, "In Torrance Police Dept., Forensics Is Women's Work, *LA Times*, February 10, 2014, www

.latimes.com/local/la-me-c1-torrance-forensics-20140210-dto -htmlstory.html.

Experts can't identify, The overall emphasis on encouraging: Melissa Beattie-Moss, "Probing Question: Do Women Dominate the Field of Forensic Science?" *Penn State News*, May 7, 2013, news.psu .edu/story/276199/2013/05/07/research/probing-question -do-women-dominate-field-forensic-science.

Some experts say women tend, Women working in the field cite: Dena Potter, "More Women Examine a Career in Forensic Science," *USA Today*, August 15, 2008, http://usatoday30.usatoday.com/tech /science/2008-08-15-forensic-science-women_N.htm.

FRANCES GLESSNER LEE (1878–1962)

"delightful, clever and precocious": Glessner House Museum, www .glessnerhouse.org/Glessners.htm.

"cozy," "Monumental and fortress-like": Glessner House Museum.

"no surprise to their friends": "Asks for Divorce from Attorney Blewett Lee," *Chicago Tribune*, June 10, 1914.

"A lady doesn't go to school!": Nuwer, "Murder in Miniature," *Slate*, June 9, 2014.

He complained they often: Nuwer, "Murder in Miniature."

"For many years I have hoped": "Mrs. Lee and President Conant Are Speakers at Opening of Library," *Harvard Crimson*, May 25, 1934.

The Department of Legal Medicine was the first: Nuwer, "Murder in Miniature."

"queenly looking woman": "Top Amateur Private Eye a 70-Year-Old Grandma," *Bloomington (IL) Pantagraph*, November 27, 1949.

"Homer Cregg, Wilby Jenks": Kahn, "Murder Downsized," *New York Times*, October 7, 2004.

It took Fanny three days: Joseph Nolan, "Hobbyist Models Murders," *Salt Lake Tribune*, May 12, 1946.

"The inspector may best examine": Kahn, "Murder Downsized."

"reasonable explanation," "some obscure, overlooked detail": Gerald M. Rosberg, "A Colloquium on Violent Death Brings 30 Detectives to Harvard," *Harvard Crimson*, December 6, 1966, www.thecrimson .com/article/1966/12/6/a-colloquium-on-violent-death-brings/.

"something of small size": Merriam-Webster, "nutshell," www.merriam
-webster.com/dictionary/nutshell.

"People take them as seriously": Kahn, "Murder Downsized."

Sidebar

Some officials think we need: "How Qualified Is Your Coroner?" *Frontline.*

"crowners": "How Qualified?"

A botched death investigation: "The Real CSI: Death Detective Dysfunc-
tion," NPR, February 1, 2011, www.npr.org/2011/02/01/133301436
/the-real-csi-death-detective-dysfunction.

In 2009 the National Academy of Science: "Coroners Don't Need
Degrees to Determine Death," NPR, February 2, 2011, www
.npr.org/2011/02/02/133403760/coroners-dont-need-degrees
-to-determine-death.

LOIS GIBSON

"When the life is being": Gibson and Mills, *Faces of Evil: Kidnappers, Murderers, Rapists and the Forensic Artist Who Puts Them Behind Bars*, 28.

"pasty white" . . . *"dark eyebrows"*: Gibson and Mills, *Faces of Evil*, 28.

The description was as generic: Christy Oglesby, "Bared Bone, Tiny Body
Led to Artist's Perfect Picture," CNN, November 27, 2007, www
.cnn.com/2007/US/11/27/riley.sketch/index.html?eref=yahoo.

"Hi, my name is Lois": Gibson and Mills, *Faces of Evil*, 64.

"Come on down, girl!" Gibson and Mills, *Faces of Evil*, 64.

"No matter how": Gibson and Mills, *Faces of Evil*, 82.

"This was a chance": Gibson and Mills, *Faces of Evil*, 88.

"Tonight my drill team": Gibson and Mills, *Faces of Evil*, 216.

"restless soul find peace": Gibson and Mills, *Faces of Evil*, 6.

"I need help finding my two brothers": Gibson and Mills, *Faces of Evil*, 161.

"I've worked with," "When they do, then I have empowered": Gibson and
Mills, *Faces of Evil*, xiv.

CRISTINA PINO

"travel all over the globe," "to make a difference": Cristina Pino, e-mail to
author, January 16, 2015.

"You are a brave and intelligent woman": Pino, e-mail, January 16, 2015.

"He helped me": Pino, e-mail, January 16, 2015.

"At the beginning it was very hard": Pino, e-mail, January 16, 2015.

"on hold": Pino, e-mail, January 16, 2015.

"Cristina e-mailed regarding": Janis Cavanaugh, e-mail to author, February 11, 2015.

"It was during my time at the forensic academy": Pino, e-mail, January 16, 2015.

"Cristina is a unique individual": Cavanaugh, e-mail to author, January 29, 2015.

"I was nervous" . . . *"I was exposed to so many"*: Pino, e-mail to author, March 14, 2015.

"right-hand man": Pino, e-mail, March 14, 2015.

"A unique experience it was": Pino, e-mail, March 14, 2015.

"I observed with trepidation": Pino, e-mail, March 14, 2015.

"It was with them": Pino, e-mail, March 14, 2015.

"I strongly believe": Pino, e-mail, January 16, 2015.

"Without any doubts": Pino, e-mail, January 16, 2015.

"It changed the way I see": Pino, e-mail, January 16, 2015.

"Working in this field": Pino, e-mail, January 16, 2015.

"I look for any signs": Pino, e-mail, March 6, 2015.

"I usually use a ruler": Pino, e-mail, March 6, 2015.

"This is a crucial aspect": Pino, e-mail, March 6, 2015.

"When I find prints": Pino, e-mail, March 6, 2015.

She uses a $1.5 million laboratory: Larry Altman, "New Lab Will Help Torrance Police Nab Criminals," *Los Angeles Daily Breeze*, October 30, 2013, www.dailybreeze.com/government-and-politics/20131030/new-lab-will-help-torrance-police-nab-criminals.

"I had to remind myself": Pino, e-mail, January 16, 2015.

"My main concern, as a foreigner": Pino, e-mail, January 16, 2015.

"After my testimony": Pino, e-mail, January 16, 2015.

"Some scenes can affect your mind": Pino, e-mail, January 16, 2015.

"When you choose this career: Pino, e-mail, January 16, 2015.

"I always feel excited": Pino, e-mail, January 16, 2015.

"This career required": Pino, e-mail, January 16, 2015.

BIBLIOGRAPHY

· · · · · · · · · · · · · · · ·

BOOKS

Appier, Janis. *Policing Women: The Sexual Politics of Law Enforcement and the LAPD*. Philadelphia: Temple University Press, 1998.

Bultema, James A. *Guardians of Angels: A History of the Los Angeles Police Department*. West Conshohocken, PA: Infinity, 2013.

Duffin, Allan T. *History in Blue: 160 Years of Women Police, Sheriffs, Detectives, and State Troopers*. Los Angeles: Duffin Creative, 2012.

Gibson, Lois, and Mills, Deanie Francis. *Faces of Evil: Kidnappers, Murderers, Rapists and the Forensic Artist Who Puts Them Behind Bars*. Liberty Corner, NJ: New Horizon, 2005.

Harrington, Penny. *Triumph of Spirit: An Autobiography by Penny Harrington*. Chicago: Brittany, 1999.

O'Hare, Sheila, and Dick, Alphild. *Wicked Denver: Mile-High Misdeeds and Malfeasance*. Charleston: History Press, 2012.

Rider, Eugene F. *The Denver Police Department: An Administrative, Organization and Operational History, 1858–1905*. Ann Arbor, MI: University Microfilms International, 1987.

Schulz, Dorothy Moses. *From Social Worker to Crimefighter: Women in United States Municipal Policing*. Westport, CT: Praeger, 1995.

Snow, Robert L. *Policewomen Who Made History: Breaking Through the Ranks*. Lanham, MD: Rowman & Littlefield, 2010.

Sullivan, Mary. *My Double Life*. New York: Farrar & Rinehart, 1938.

Wallace, William. *Michelangelo: the Artist, the Man, and his Times*. New York: Cambridge University Press, 2010.

Wells, Sandra, and Alt, Betty. *Policewomen: Life with the Badge*. Westport, CT: Praeger, 2005.

NEWSPAPERS AND MAGAZINES

"All Pleaded Not Guilty." *Omaha Daily Bee*, August 31, 1894.

"Chicanery." *Rocky Mountain News*, August 31, 1894.

"Criminals Have Little Love for This Woman." *Detroit Free Press*, June 3, 1908.

Davis, Cecile. "Washington, by Citywide Effort, Cuts Down Juvenile Delinquency." *Atlanta Constitution*, July 15, 1945.

Dille, Marie. "LA 1st City in World to Establish City Mothers." *Altoona (PA) Tribune*, February 2, 1916.

"Educating the Women Prisoners." *Salem (OR) Daily Capital Journal*, April 4, 1910.

"Emotional Girls Warned Not to Go to Washington." *Tipton (VA) Tribune*, June 10, 1942.

"Fears War as Morals Get Looser." *Washington Times*, July 4, 1921.

Finder, Alan. "The Subway Crash." *New York Times*, August 29, 1991. www.nytimes.com/1991/08/29/nyregion/subway-crash-irt-driver-charged-5-deaths-crash-shuts-line-ties-up-city.html.

"The First Municipal Woman Detective in the World." *New York Times*, March 3, 1912.

"First Negro Policewoman Joined LA Force in 1916." *Ebony Magazine*, September 1954.

"Five Now Held as Taxi Robbers; One Tells Whole Plot." *New York Tribune*, January 28, 1912.

"Her Ears Hear Women's Woes," *LA Times*, October 4, 1914.

"How Qualified Is Your Coroner?" *Frontline*. www.pbs.org/wgbh /pages/frontline/post-mortem/things-to-know/how-qualified-is -your-coroner.html.

"In the Interest of Delicacy." *New York Times*, May 12, 1882.

Kahn, Eve. "Murder Downsized." *New York Times*, October 7, 2004.

"Mrs. Goodwin Nabs a Spook." *New York Times*, May 11, 1913.

Newberry, Laura. "Meet the Chief: Northampton's Capt. Jody Kasper Credits Guidance Counselor for Her Career." *Mass Live*, June 25, 2015. www.masslive.com/news/index.ssf/2015/06 /meet_the_chief_northamptons_jo.html.

"New York's Only Woman Detective." *Spanish American*, May 25, 1912.

Nuwer, Rachel. "Murder in Miniature." *Slate*, June 9, 2014. www .slate.com/articles/health_and_science/science/2014/06/nutshell _dioramas_of_death_frances_glessner_lee_forensic_science _and_training.html.

"Police Stations in Chicago Are Lousy." *Chicago Day Book*, September 21, 1915.

"Police Woman Thwarts Runaway Romance." *San Francisco Chronicle*, September 2, 1912.

"Policewoman Grace Wilson Shows Mettle." *Chicago Defender*, November 2, 1918.

"Portland's Tarnished Penny." *Time*, April 14, 1986.

Price, Gertrude M. "'City Mother' Dispenses Love to All in Trouble." *Santa Cruz Evening News*, December 22, 1914.

Ragsdale, Eleanor. "Capital's Juvenile Delinquents Give No. 1 Police-women Headaches." *Pampa (TX) Daily News*, July 27, 1942.

"Raid by Policewomen." *Washington Post*, March 3, 1919.

"Sexless Man Is Arrested." *Wichita Daily Eagle*, September 12, 1915.

"She Is a Police Commissioner." *Boston Daily Globe*, June 10, 1894.

Sibley, Celestine. "Policewomen Nip Crime in Bud." *Atlanta Constitution*, April 6, 1950.

"Swearing in of Northampton Chief of Police Jody Kasper." YouTube video. July 1, 2015. www.youtube.com/watch?v=peUnCup TWQU.

"They Start with Crime as Children." *Atlanta Constitution*, April 6, 1950.

"War Makes Heroes Out of Some People but Others Turn Out to Be Shoplifters." *Rio Grande Valley (TX) Morning Star,* January 16, 1944.

"Woman Made Municipal Detective." *Meriden (CT) Morning Record,* March 2, 1912.

WEBSITES

"About Julia." True North Focus: www.truenorthfocus.com/About _Julia.html.

"Village History." The Greenwich Village Society For Historic Preservation: www.gvshp.org/_gvshp/resources/history.htm.

"Virtual Tour." Glessner House Museum: www.glessnerhouse.org /VirtualTour.htm

Woman's Christian Temperance Union: www.wctu.org.

INDEX